Everything You wanted to ask a psychologist

Frequently Asked Questions and Answers

Arthur Hill & Oswald Howard

ISBN: 9798655442009

PREFACE

Learn to live in comfort and pleasure with yourself, then your partner will be well next to you.

Friendship is an important close relationship, even in adulthood. Each person must have at least two close friends. If you have one friend - this is happiness, two - it's wonderful, and three - you are truly a rich man!

As a rule, in relationships (if they are not rigid, not frozen), the value orientations of friends change in turn. This does not mean at all that in this situation one takes the initiative, and the next time takes another. Sometimes one of the friends can take an initiative position for years, then there is a quarrel or a quarrel, a long break, and only then the second friend begins to get involved in the situation, realizing that for him the relationship is important and it is time to take the initiative into his own hands.

Some borderline reactions are characteristic of each of us (relatively speaking, any healthy neurotic) - we sometimes react painfully to certain situations, and in difficult periods of life we may even end up in the borderline zone of our psyche organization.

The first and most important thing to learn is to monitor your behavior when you get into a merger. Ideally, it is better to have a close friend or psychotherapist who knows you well and pays attention to excessive merging with a partner ("It seems to me that you are too close, you need to move a little away!").

Procrastination is a tendency to constantly postpone things "for later" (including important and urgent ones!). This condition becomes a real problem when a person is in it most of the time - constant "breakdowns" of planned affairs, poor-quality result and, as a result, stress, guilt, troubles and missed opportunities.

Depression is a mental disorder characterized by depressed mood, loss of strength, fatigue and loss of interest in everything. Starting with seemingly simple symptoms of sleep disturbance and poor appetite, this condition quickly becomes a cause of interruptions with neurotransmitters, blocks the synthesis of serotonin and dopamine, over time you will be visited more often by bad thoughts, overcome laziness and unwillingness to do anything, apathy will awaken and lethargy.

Envy is a feeling that is customary to condemn, to be ashamed of, and not even admit to oneself in it. However, in reality, there are no bad feelings - they all signal to us something important.

Contents

How to make peace? How to return the relationship?
How to fall in love with anyone?
How to regain trust after treason?
How to determine in communication that you are communicating with a borderline person?
How not to depend on a relationship?
How to drive a man crazy in 2 minutes?
How to restore self-esteem after treason?
How to get rid of love addiction?
How to deal with procrastination?
How to overcome laziness?
How to develop willpower?
How to overcome shame?
How to drive a woman crazy in 2 minutes?
How to prevent treason?
How to increase self-esteem and stop being comfortable?
How to increase self-esteem after the betrayal of a husband / wife?
How to love yourself?
How not to depend on the opinions of others?
How to deal with perfectionism?
How to stop envy?
How to survive treason, betrayal, loss and start living?
How to identify a liar?
How to protect yourself from aggression?
How to return sex to a long relationship?
How to overcome the fear of rejection?
How to keep a relationship happy?
How to find peace of mind?
How to find your meaning in life?
How to understand that you feel sorry for yourself?
How to find friends?
How not to be nervous when you are late?
How to deal with anxiety?
How to get rid of chronic fatigue?
How to quickly get out of depression?
How to stop being a victim?
How to deal with unpleasant feelings?
How to understand what is behind desires?
How to be full?
How to decide on a change in life?

How to stop getting hung up on marriage, marriage, marriage?

Quite often, this issue is of interest to young people (both girls and boys). Will I have a family? Will I meet exactly the girl that I will like? Such experiences are quite natural! But how to let go of the situation of marriage and stop thinking about possible loneliness?

This topic worries more people at a young age, because they do not have enough experience in relationships (against the background of a hormonal surge, they really want to establish relationships with the opposite sex, but they did not encounter all the difficulties in a couple). Often the level of anxiety decreases when we find the desired partner (I have a man / woman). Direct formalization of relations currently excites few. Basically, a feeling of anxiety arises from the need to be in a relationship, due to the unconscious instinctive need to meet "your" person (we all want to feel warmth, comfort, tenderness, etc.).

The next age category, prone to such experiences, is people aged 30-40 years. Here is another reason - anxiety for their status in society. In our society, an unwritten rule is accepted - if you have a man, then you are a normal woman. A similar situation is with the opposite sex, but in men this condition manifests itself closer to 40 years ("I am a normal man, because I have a wife!").

In fact, anxiety and anxiety about status have rather deep psychological roots. This is a low self-esteem, derogatory feeling "I - under-!" (not good enough, not normal enough, unworthy if it does not meet the generally accepted requirements and criteria in society). If you have anxiety about the meeting of "your" person, you should carefully analyze all the accompanying factors. There is an unconscious need for marriage, living together with a partner, presenting your status to others ("Look, I have a wife / husband!") - you have problems with self-esteem. As a rule, such people cannot respect themselves for their virtues and positive qualities ("I'm quite a normal person! I'm fine with me, and I don't need any confirmation of status!"), Do not approve of their behavior and actions (in a projective way through other people, believing that others think badly of them). How to deal with anxiety associated with low self-esteem? Move the focus of attention from other people to yourself - become a worthy person for yourself. It is that worthy person whom you dream to meet. We always meet a partner on the principle of psychological development, and your level will be approximately the same. What does this mean? If you constantly meet unworthy people, then you have a lot of bugs inside. Thus, your psyche is trying to signal: "Please help me, correct me!". Another person is always a mirror for us, and no matter how it seems to us that something is wrong with your partner, he is angry and aggressive, reconcile yourself to the fact that there is just as much negative inside your unconscious!

Start with your development. Do something exciting, just love life next to your partner (or without). In such situations, it is very important to get a sense of dignity and respect for yourself, to have a favorite thing (it's not necessary to go into it with your head, it's quite enough to give it half an hour a day, but you need to understand that this is exactly what "gives birth" to light within you, inspires, makes you move on). And even one favorite hobby will put you an order of magnitude higher in relation to competitors. Ask yourself a direct question: "What is worse for me - to live my whole life alone or to live a life with an unloved person?" The experience of not meeting "your" person makes many people engage in relations with the wrong people. If you understand for yourself and decide that "it's better to do it yourself, and not with anyone", it will be much easier for you to live, the level of anxiety will decrease, and you can enter into a relationship with great dignity. What will happen to you if in your whole life you cannot meet "your" person?

Suppose you are destined to live up to 90, 100, 120 years, and you live life alone. What will happen to you? How will you feel? What will you do? Can you handle it? If you can't cope, and the anxiety is so strong that there is a strong uncontrollable fear, you should visit a therapist. In this state, a person's internal negative is brewing, and he definitely will not be able to meet "his" person. The therapist will help you work out the trauma of attachment. That is why when you can honestly and positively answer all questions ("I feel comfortable and so!"), You will live and enjoy every day spent, work, develop, communicate with friends, relax, pay attention to some interests in life, you will become interesting to others, and your circle of potential partners will expand significantly. As a rule, when the tension in the zone "Oh God, I want a relationship, I want a family!" Decreases, the right person appears nearby. And then it's completely irrelevant - the official registration of marriage or not, you just feel good together.

Learn to live in comfort and pleasure with yourself, then your partner will be well next to you.

How to restore intimacy in a relationship?

95% emotional closeness in a relationship solves all problems in a couple. How to restore emotional closeness between partners? The first and most important point is whether there is a trusting dialogue between you and your partner? It is confidential, and not communication, when you throw insults, accusations, demands at each other, communicate some expectations. Confidential dialogue implies a deep conversation between partners when you share your feelings and feelings. If you understand that over a long time resentment, feelings, unspoken anger have accumulated, and in general the relationship has practically collapsed, this is a signal to a regular "negotiation table" with a partner (at least once a week, discuss what does not suit you and who). However, it is important here not to blame a loved one, not to attack him so that he has to defend himself against you, but to build a dialogue so that he hears and understands your pain.

Listen to your partner and hear his pain, understand what painful points you could touch. Your task in this dialogue is, first of all, to understand the loved one, and then bear your pain. When one of you takes the first step, the second will reach for it (agree, it will be difficult not to hear you in response if you heard the partner's pain). And here it is important to say: "Sorry, I'm sorry that you took my words this way. I didn't mean it at all and didn't want to hurt you. "I don't think the fault lies with me, but I fully understand your pain." Learn to share with your partner experienced child injuries and thereby explain why this is how you reacted to the moment when he was going to hurt you. Only in this way will you be able to treat a loved one with great understanding and next time keep silent in a similar situation (or you will not use painful phrases to smooth out a conversation). In fact, everything happens on the machine, if you realize what kind of mines you're attacking in your soul.

Develop the ability to simultaneously hear and talk about your feelings, injuries, experiences. This is intimacy, when you let a person into your soul, you can look into it and not get lost there, not merge with it, not absorb one another, but hear, understand and model the behavior of each of you in the following similar situation. An important point - each of the partners should have no belief that the other will not understand, not hear, he does not care. No, it is not! And if you have confidence that the partner is able to hear, you will speak, then the dialogue will be built by itself.

Communication is also creativity, you need to be able to adapt to a partner, adapt to various situations. At some points, a person can be very vulnerable, at some less - and this is a different model of behavior (somewhere a joke will come up, and somewhere a comic remark will cause deep resentment). That is why be extremely attentive to the partner and to what is happening in his inner life. A couple is the ability to share inner life, hear and notice it. Relationship support. You must always support each other.

Remember that in relationships, each of us is as vulnerable as children are, and any word can hurt a partner in the heart and settle deep in the soul. Be careful in your statements, in evaluating a loved one. If a partner complains, shares difficulties, first of all support him, even if you see that he is wrong in working relationships (for example, he had a fight with colleagues, considers them idiots): "I sympathize that this is happening in your life. It's a pity that the team is so strange and unshaken, and reacts in this way. " Of course, if you notice his true behavior, it should be said about the energy that he brings to the working relationship, but this is best done when the partner directly takes an interest in you, tormented by constantly unpleasant situations: "Well, why? Why is everything repeated at every new workplace? " ("Are you ready to hear the answer? It will be a bit of criticism. Are you ready to hear it now?"). Ask the person directly if he can perceive the truth - perhaps, in this case, on the contrary, he wants to hear words of comfort because of his emotional state ("Tell me everything when I am ready!").

You can still talk about this topic with your partner when he is the most resourceful, he is in a good mood, but even in this case you should start gently ("Regarding your working relationship with colleagues ... I thought for a long time, and I have something to say, but this "It will be rather unpleasant to hear. Do you want to hear my feedback? Maybe you will take my words into account, or you may spit them out without thinking about anything - your right." Understand for yourself that all this is done to support the partner and not in order to show him: "Yeah, you're like that with me, you're behaving like that!" This is a way to nowhere, and you shouldn't ruin your relationship, because the response will certainly be (if not explicitly, then in in the form of passive aggression after some time.)

Put the relationship in the foreground - only in this case you will always look for ways to make peace with a partner, improve the relationship in a couple and make them closer. However, do not be fanatical about it! If you constantly push on close of the first person ("Let's be close, let's talk openly more often!"), this causes some rejection. Every day, no relationship will be able to talk about any problems, so sometimes pause, swallow grievances, endure at some moments, start keeping a personal diary, go to a psychologist - you need to learn to contain your feelings; and at that moment when the partner will be ready to listen to everything, talk with him. In addition, it is very important not to merge with the opinions of others regarding your loved one, this mistake is quite common, especially among girls. For example, some friend or even mother told you that men don't behave like that, this is not a man's act. As a result, someone else's outlook on life becomes more priority for you than the beliefs of your husband, and this really hurts the male half.

There may be another situation where men are very emotionally merged with their mother (in the morning he wakes up and immediately calls, calls and reports during the day, where he was and what he did), then the woman has a feeling of "third superfluous", as if the couple also lives with partner's mom. Put in the background the opinions of sisters, brothers, uncles and aunts, they should not fall within the boundaries of your relationship. Relationships are you and the partner! Set clear and secure boundaries that each of you must adhere to (violate - problems arise). Talking about support will be useless if a loved one feels that you are including someone else and someone else's opinion is more important than your own.

Relationships in a pair are not always joyful and happy - if you feel good together most of the time, this is already wonderful. To ask for support and comfort is quite normal, every partner has the right to do so. However, often when we complain to relatives, friends (all those who are our resource and support) about our soul mate, we only say bad things about the person, and good things are missed (go complaining about my husband is the norm, but they praised for cleaning the apartment hardly anyone can). As a rule, in such situations, our resource person also forgets to think about a quarrel in the family today, and tomorrow you will hug and forget about the negative - usually these things are not accepted to discuss. That is why you should not pay attention to the opinions of other people about your husband, protect him (even from others!) - yes, today he did not do very well, but in general he remained a wonderful person.

How to make peace? How to return the relationship?

Friendship is an important close relationship, even in adulthood. Each person must have at least two close friends. If you have one friend - this is happiness, two - it's wonderful, and three - you are truly a rich man! Sometimes situations arise when a person, having many friends, quarrels or for some unknown reason ceases to communicate with one of them, and begins to get bored. What to do in this case? It's scary to take the initiative, but he suddenly rejects it, but deep down in his mind, constant thoughts about the situation do not leave him alone.

There is a rather interesting theory - if you think about someone, that someone also thinks about you. As a rule, in 80% of cases this is confirmed in life. That is why it is likely that your friend is also sad that you broke up. However, the reason why communication ceased became "across the throat". Do not be a proud and arrogant person, do not be afraid to seem stupid - call a friend to meet and take a direct look at what happened in your relationship ("Why did we quarrel? Why did we quarrel?"). If the quarrel is related to specific circumstances, it is important that you understand both yours and his part of the guilt. It's necessary not only to strive to make claims ("Well, you didn't listen to me when I needed it! Everything, now I won't communicate with you!"), Understand your behavior! It is likely that in your actions there was a hidden subtext that transmitted to a person a rejection, some kind of neglect or indifference.

Try to recall the situation "in terms of personnel", analyze your words and actions, think about what has happened in your relationship lately, because of which you could offend your friend. Be honest and straightforward towards yourself (especially if friendships have developed over the years - for example, classmates, a kindergarten, etc.). Understand that this is a person who has witnessed a huge part of your life, he knows you as you really are - in our time it is very valuable and important!

So, allow yourself to be vulnerable with someone close to you, as much as possible in your situation. Try to open up and look at the response. If a person is angry with you, begins to stomp on sore spots, be honest with him ("Because of anger you are making me even more painful now! Do you really want us to stop talking?"). If you ask direct specific questions, sooner or later, the interlocutor will misfire and understand that he is doing nonsense (especially if the relationship is long and valuable for you and your friend).

I want to give as an example the situation that happened to my good friend. He quarreled with a friend, although they were friends since school. Friends see each other quite often (they meet almost every evening, go to visit each other, help in all matters, do massages, etc.). And so, one of the friends openly cheated on the other, and although it was not pleasant for a comrade, he tried to get closer after a while (instead of a frank conversation, he sent some photos to a friend). Direct contact with the offender was difficult for him ("Offended me, how am I going to be the first to reconcile ?! Suddenly, next time you will do the same to me?"). What was the real reason for the quarrel? Fatigue from constant intimacy with a friend! To some extent, personal boundaries were violated, I wanted to take a break in relations (metaphorically - a person overeat, and he feels bad), but a friend could not say so directly ("Listen, I need time to take a break from our relationship! Let's take a break") It is a break in contact that will allow you to rethink a lot for you and your friend.

The time to rethink the situation as a whole is priceless, and you should not be afraid of this period. It is after such interruptions that some miraculous transformations of a person take place, initially rejecting this connection, devaluing your relationship and showing aggression. Often there are people who, having something in life, do not value it, and having lost it, they suddenly begin to understand how good it was. Give your friend time, do not put pressure on him with love and fear of loss, but be sure to label yourself ("I am, and I would like to make peace with you. When you are ready, let's talk.") Speak directly with a friend ("Even now, when we talked, I still think that you were wrong last time!"). Remember: the first to come to terms is not the one who is wrong, but the one for whom relations are more valuable.

As a rule, in relationships (if they are not rigid, not frozen), the value orientations of friends change in turn. This does not mean at all that in this situation one takes the initiative, and the next time takes another. Sometimes one of the friends can take an initiative position for years, then there is a quarrel or a quarrel, a long break, and only then the second friend begins to get involved in the situation, realizing that for him the relationship is important and it is time to take the initiative into his own hands. However, often the second does not have time inside the consciousness to understand the value of the relationship, if the first goes to reconciliation too quickly, so do not rush, give yourself a break, slowly build the relationship. As a rule, everything that is done quickly is of poor quality; and everything that is done slowly has a great chance of becoming important, strong and valuable.

How to fall in love with anyone?

There is an interesting psychological method that allows you to "fall in love with a person", called the "Mexican soul."

This principle was first described by American psychologists during a study of Latin American marriages. The scheme works almost always if it is correctly applied, but the approach to neurotics is more effective. The technique includes three stages - acquaintance, rejection, rapprochement.

The first phase should be bright for your partner - you need to make it clear to the person that he is special, to help him experience the full range of emotions and experiences near you, to inspire confidence that he will not have such an emotional storm with anyone else. You can also show your originality, but you need to know yourself very well (you can not talk about this, the main thing is to be confident in yourself and your merits, then your internal state will be broadcast without any words). At the first stage, it is important to give a person a feeling of complete merger and involvement - listen, be interested, show curiosity, open up a little by yourself, find joint activities. The more compatibility you have, the stronger the feeling of merging and understanding. If the partner sympathizes with you, or you know how to adapt, you tend to fall into co-dependence, the use of this technique will not cause additional difficulties, otherwise you will have to learn.

At the rejection stage, it is necessary to sharply create a distance, find a plausible reason and refuse to request the next meeting, miss a phone call or call back in an hour and a half (work, shower, household chores, etc.), but be sure to give hope for a continued relationship. You do not need to regularly repel a partner - do this once or twice. The rejection phase does not have to be painful. Relations are built on the principle of "cold and hot souls", and on this contrast a person "pours" into contact, respectively, he has a feeling of guilt and shame, a sense of worthlessness arises inside his mind ("What have I done wrong?") And how consequence, I want to return my partner ("I want to return those wonderful and warm feelings that I experienced next to this person!").

The next stage is rapprochement. Each next meeting, get closer a little more to "fix on yourself" a person, while moving away from each other less. We alternate the last two phases - 3-4 dates for rapprochement, 1 for rejection ("Sorry, I am extremely happy with you, but I need to urgently run away!").

It is very important that everything happens naturally, without stress. Some people may have a problem with the rejection phase, especially those who are prone to co-dependence and fall in love easily. What to do in this case? Your life should be in full swing - get busy, do not think about a partner, completely disconnect from the situation that excites you. If you still get involved in a relationship, it's difficult for you to control yourself, ask a close friend / girlfriend for an urgent meeting. An interesting point is that people who tend to focus on the state of merger often come across daffodil partners who easily lose the rejection phase (sometimes even ahead of schedule). As a result, they are embroiled in a peculiar game - who will be the first to be more indifferent to get out of the merger? However, you should use your advantage wisely - do not be daffodils, do not hurt other people. If you want to "play", make two or three circles according to the scheme and stop - you do not need to fall in love with a person who is not interesting to you. If there is sympathy, at some point the game will cease to seem important, projections that require explanation will appear in the relationship, it will take a lot of energy, and resentment will accumulate. A narcissistically equipped person will remain silent, fall in love, idealize you, but then devaluation and disappointment will follow.

All insults will be remembered, and aggression will accumulate, and at a certain moment everything will splash out. That is why you should not abuse the affection of another, play only in the flirting zone.

How to regain trust after treason?

You have decided to forgive the betrayal of your partner, but inside your mind you have difficulty trusting this man / woman. What to do in this situation?

Lack of trust in the case of betrayal (anyone - a partner, friend, native person) is a completely normal state. Trust is, first and foremost, positive relationships between people, an expression of true feelings and emotions, confidence in the actions and decency of another person. This "narrow bridge" is being built for a long time, you need to try and invest in each other in order to learn to trust.

If we talk about the loss of trust and about you, as the injured party, at this moment you are experiencing a sense of injustice - you tried, put your heart and soul into relationships, made some efforts, and in return you got a betrayal. It turns out that all efforts were in vain. The question arises - is it worth trusting yourself and your choice (who to believe and who not)?

Ask yourself this, go to a consultation with a psychologist. Perhaps you really have an inadequate idea of what trust is (numerous stories of women who get into relationships with psychopaths and men who are manipulated in relationships testify to this) - in this case, you need to find out why this happens.

There are also reverse situations - you trusted a completely normal person, nothing portended trouble, but suddenly your trust was trampled and betrayed. So, how to deal with the gnawing feeling inside and learn to believe again? Forgive yourself (you trusted the wrong person, did not notice the unspoken signs of future betrayal). Make conclusions - carefully analyze the situation, find out what exactly you can get out of it (In which cases, you should be more attentive to the actions of your husband? Should I run after him, checking every step, messages on the phone, etc.? At what points do you need to pay more attention to your partner in order to avoid a repetition of an unpleasant situation?). This is a kind of work on mistakes, but do not take responsibility and shoulder the blame for everything that happens. The blame lies not only with you - understand and accept this fact.

Work out in detail your mistakes and partner's mistakes, discuss all the negative aspects ("Do you agree that you were wrong here? And in this situation I was wrong").

So, to restore confidence, the following factors are very important: - time; - the desire of a partner; - communication with a partner. If you decide to forgive your partner after the betrayal, keep in mind that this period will be a crisis for your couple.

However, it is possible that such a situation will bring your feelings back to life, you will begin to understand each other's needs and desires, and you will become closer. Often people hold a grudge for many years. This is a peculiar way of manipulating a partner, but in the end, such a technique will not lead to anything good - repeated betrayal, breakdown of relations or complete separation of the partner (bodily a person will be in a relationship, but not emotionally). What can be done so that resentment does not accumulate? Assign the price of punishment to your partner (How can he (she) atone for his guilt?), For example, let him bring flowers every two days for six months (be sure to indicate the time). It is important to listen to yourself - the idea should come from the depths of the heart.

You can make a list of desired actions on the part of the partner (buying jewelry with diamonds, a trip abroad for a vacation, etc.). In some situations, it is enough to take only the emotional component (for example, every night for a month, the partner should give you 15-30 minutes and be your psychologist - listen, communicate). After the partner fulfills his "punishment", forget the painful situation and forgive him. People who are obsessed with insult can take a great psychological approach in a playful way - take a piece of paper and write a receipt about the obligation to forgive the partner and never to remember it again. Usually, a person is ready for such a ritual only a month after the betrayal of a loved one. Such a deadline is quite acceptable - trust is not restored quickly, give yourself time, and let the partner be patient, because now you will carefully check it. And talk to each other about it!

How to determine in communication that you are communicating with a borderline person?

 Some borderline reactions are characteristic of each of us (relatively speaking, any healthy neurotic) - we sometimes react painfully to certain situations, and in difficult periods of life we may even end up in the borderline zone of our psyche organization.

So, painful behavior with a manifestation of emotional instability, impulsivity and a strong level of desocialization is inherent in any person, can begin to manifest itself in youth and arise in a variety of situations. The only difference is that a healthy person has a number of compensatory mechanisms, adapted to reality and often used.

A person with a borderline organization of personality, on the contrary, practically does not possess the skills of using secondary protective mechanisms. In addition, the compensatory component of his structure is completely different - all thoughts are voiced. All symptoms of a borderline personality are well represented in Otto F. Kernberg's book, "Severe Personality Disorders."

In general, you can recognize yourself in each of the items below, but it's worth considering how much all this interferes with your environment and loved ones, how often do such reactions occur?

What are the signs to determine the borderline personality in communication? Speech is easiest to notice when in contact with a person. Due to confused identity and rather weak contact with reality, the first signs of a borderline personality appear in a conversation. How is this expressed? A person initially does not mention the participation of a third party in a certain situation, but then casually refers to him in a conversation. At this moment, the interlocutor, because of the speaker's fragmented speech, unconsciously feels that he was inattentive and missed something from what was said, respectively, he unconsciously takes the blame. An extremely fragmented identity leads to fragmented phrases and confused presentation of events in speech - what happens inside is reflected outside, there can be no other options.

Often, it is the ability to speak that allows us to understand what is happening in a person's soul.

Persons with a borderline organization of the psyche add many details to the overall story, sometimes from completely different areas. That is why the interlocutor has the impression that he is inattentively listening, as a result of which he has an internal tension: "How can I be even more careful ?!" Sometimes large pieces are missed in the story, for the borderline personality this is the norm - due to the lack of contact with reality, a person believes that everything is clear to the interlocutor ("I understand everything!"). The reaction of affects, especially to anxiety and frustration. For example, a wife may not like that her husband returned home 10 minutes later than promised. As a result, she sets up a grand scandal and takes things out into the corridor. Anger can last for 2 hours or several days (in rare situations; usually a flash of indignation blinds a person for a short while, and he calms down). In fact, the borderline person is very tired of this behavior.

However, people in this state cannot withstand anxiety and, accordingly, fight frustration. What does this mean? A person has desires and inner needs, but the world dictates to him completely different living conditions, those around him live their own lives and do not think only about him. As a rule, frustration occurs when one wants someone to fulfill their wishes. Having been refused, the borderline person shows a high level of anger, uses other protection mechanisms (isolation, rejection, acting out or rejection of advancing), sometimes he uses rather primitive manipulations against the background of anxiety ("Do this!", "Do not do this!", "Do not I'll talk to you! "," I'm offended! "etc.). Instant contradictory attitude to yourself. Due to diffuse identity, a person does not understand in general who he is. As a result, his self-image depends solely on those around him, his mood, his state of frustration, anxiety, etc. How is this manifested?

The borderline person has a great mood - "I am so young! And he did so much! " After a few minutes, or, for example, the next day - "No, well, I'm dumb! Anyway, nothing works for me! " It is important to understand that this is not a manipulation, a person really thinks about himself at the moment. The presence of primitive defenses (or first-order defenses) - idealization, depreciation, isolation, strong splitting (here I am good, but bad here), omnipotence or just control (a person wants to feel that everything is in his hands, he is completely in control of information and manages all), projective identification (for example, the interlocutor feels the whole spectrum of emotions that the borderline personality does not want to recognize and denies - anger, etc.). Protection mechanisms are mainly used in times of anxiety, severe frustration or in painful situations - thus, people with a borderline organization of the psyche are protected from the world. What if the loved one is a borderline person?

Do not be scared! This "symptom" is not transmitted by airborne droplets. The very essence of the borderline personality is that the core of the psyche itself is broken and fragmented. In fact, this is a mature adult who has experienced severe psychological trauma at an early age.

Remember that the ego of this person is very weak, so be lenient towards him.

Do not label your loved ones!

Do not independently diagnose their psyche and make diagnoses! First of all, this is a stalemate for you - it will be difficult for you to live with this information.

Treat loved ones as people with their own difficulties. Remember: if they hurt you, they have a strange and inadequate reaction to your actions or words, this is due to the experienced anxiety and fear arising from the inability to cope with frustration. Respect these feelings! Talk more. If a person with a borderline organization of personality has a rather high level of intelligence, you can reach his consciousness without psychotherapy.

The main thing is to understand whether he is ready to discuss his reaction with outsiders. Do not force to attend psychotherapy sessions, conduct introspection, read special literature, go to trainings or watch webinars while sitting at home. For all this, a person's desire is needed, otherwise you will receive a negative response to all attempts. The borderline person most of all wants to be accepted as she is - this is the most important aspect of their psyche.

How not to depend on a relationship?

How to choose the most comfortable distance of merger and freedom in a relationship? How to overcome the crazy fear of merging, losing yourself and your borders?

The first and most important thing to learn is to monitor your behavior when you get into a merger. Ideally, it is better to have a close friend or psychotherapist who knows you well and pays attention to excessive merging with a partner ("It seems to me that you are too close, you need to move a little away!").

What might the merger look like?

You constantly go after your partner, do all his work, you can't think and talk about anything else. In order to get out of the state of merger, not to be afraid of closeness with a partner, to feel confident on its territory and not to be afraid to invite your own, you need to know and be able to defend your borders (at least once in your life you need to separate from those people on whom you depended before or still dependent (e.g. separation from parents)).

Having experienced the separation process with your parents, you will understand at what stage your merger has become excessive and you need to move away from your partner, and you can easily take a step back. At this stage, it is important to tell a loved one that you are incredibly comfortable and well in merging with him, but you begin to lose yourself as a person, so you need time to be alone, to restore your internal resources. Convince your partner that you will definitely return after you come to your senses. Schedule your next appointment.

If you are a counter-dependent person and are desperately afraid of this merger, as a rule, you will have a relationship with a co-dependent person. Such people have an instinctive feeling of anxiety that they will abandon him. They are afraid of losing attachment and being left alone, so they quickly become attached to their partner and begin to worry that some kind of disaster will happen if you step back at least a step. Accordingly, by agreeing on the next meeting, you slightly reduce their anxiety - a person knows about the meeting, is sure that everything will be fine then, and he only needs to survive this period of forced loneliness. Give yourself the right to live in a relationship freely, to be yourself, not to lose your worldview and life values.

Find a person with whom you share spiritual and intellectual values and life views; someone who really believes that you need to be alone for a week with your thoughts, and not just agree to tolerate your absence. A close person should not be afraid that for a while he will be alone. This does not "knock" him out of contact ("You know, I want to stay one day or two" - "That's it, you don't love me. For now"), he is quite adequate to your decision ("Yes, I understand everything. U I also have things that I can do while you sort out your thoughts. ") Partners must have an interesting and eventful life separately from each other, sometimes get saved by work (if you see that your thoughts are fixated on one thing, go headlong into working issues). Everything is simple - work in any incomprehensible life situation! It really helps. In addition, you will get rid of harmful thoughts, and you can build a career.

Do not limit your social circle - communicate with friends, come to visit them, meet somewhere and share your thoughts. In any case, your hormones make you dream about a partner, remember the beautiful and warm moments of the last meeting and think about the next. Friends can rejoice for you if everything is fine in the relationship, and support when necessary.

We are all social beings, and friendly communication will allow us to unload our psyche a little and breathe a sigh of relief. Tens of thousands of processes take place inside our minds, hundreds of thoughts flash, and all this at some point rolls like a snowball and worsens the emotional state. By sharing with someone, we reduce internal stress - this is the law of psychology, indestructible, like the laws of physics! Have a hobby and devote free time to this occupation.

The important point is to choose those interests that you can really get carried away, and if you go deeper, you won't be able to think about anything else (or your thoughts will be in free flight - light, pleasant and unobtrusive). When your hands are busy, your head is resting, but you continue to think about issues that are disturbing you, but this happens as in a dream - thoughts themselves are "laid out on the shelves".

Learn to rely on your feelings and desires so that you do not lose yourself when you merge with a partner. I always want to make it pleasant for a loved one, spend free time together ... But you have your own desires and feelings that you sacrifice for the sake of relations! Eat, take a walk, meet friends, lie on the beach, go somewhere ...

Do not forget to realize your desires and needs, do not focus only on what is connected with the partner. Another important point - give yourself the right to have a strong relationship, but be a free person. Believe me, this option is quite acceptable and exists! Today, there is a pronounced trend of free relations - partners agree among themselves about this, and most often girls are the initiator of such freedom. Paradoxically, in our time, men want to get married, and women prefer personal independence. By implying freedom of relationship, this is not about outside relationships. As a rule, people who agree do not cheat on a partner.

The second amazing trend in the modern world is that even when married and having children together, people live separately. Osho mentioned this idea, telling some story. In fact, it looks like this: you have your own home, your partner has it, and you go to visit each other (you want it for a week, you want it for longer), and the children live with their mother and father in turn. Relatively speaking, everything happens at will here and now: we want to stay together - we stayed, I want to rest from each other - we parted. For many of us, this option is completely unacceptable, but that is how the balance between merging and distance is maintained, and then additional questions do not arise. It is also very important to be able to choose the right moment for distance, taking into account not only your desires, but also the needs of your partner. In other words, it should be a joint solution. And each time - a new creative process that you create together with a loved one.

This is creativity in relationships - do you want to be as merged with your partner as possible, be alone or not communicate at all for some time (there may be a situation where you want to completely limit communication, and the partner asks you to call up once a day - and you agree: "Good. Every day, one call for 10 minutes. Satisfies?").

 Relationships are hard and difficult work that many people fear, because everyone wants us to have clearly defined rules (do it like this, and there will be happiness!). In fact, if you follow them clearly, you will become bored and uninterested in living. The more freedom in the relationship, the more you experience joy, happiness and harmony.

How to drive a man crazy in 2 minutes?

There is only one way - feel like the most attractive woman! To please a man, it's not enough just to make "lips and eyebrows". Learn to go crazy with yourself and enjoy yourself (it doesn't matter what kind of body you have, eyebrows, eyes, if there are imperfections in appearance, whether you wear sexy clothes). The important thing is how you yourself feel about yourself and how you look at the desired man. A woman who knows how to enjoy herself, knows how to enjoy her man. Men, seeing the gleam in the eyes of the fair sex, completely do not focus on her appearance (it is understood that a person has no problems with obesity, anorexia, unhealthy skin color, mental facial expressions, etc.).

In a manic state, a girl with any weight and appearance can easily seduce a man who she likes. It is all about her emotional state, incredible self-confidence and alluring sparkle in her eyes. In such a state, she feels herself "the ruler of the world", Bruce Almighty, and the whole world is right at her feet. There are exceptions - you cannot seduce absolutely any man, there are quite closed or pinched personalities that do not "turn on" when using this approach. In addition, two people participate in a relationship (even if it's just flirting), and the will of the second can not always coincide with yours. That is why you should not console yourself with the illusions that you can drive anyone crazy.

However, if you have sparkles and pleasure in your eyes, most men will surely pay attention. Flying, beautiful and feminine, or insolent and rude walk - this is absolutely unimportant! The main thing is to enjoy yourself, everything else in a general way will look quite harmonious. A man perfectly reads a woman's condition (how she relates to herself and to him), therefore, sensing vibes in relation to herself, he perceives this as a possible development of relations.

Otherwise, most men are even afraid to approach the most charming and attractive woman. Be happy that you live, you have a wonderful life, you enjoy every day, walk along the street and just sing songs in your soul - this is the state that will help you seduce the desired man!

How to restore self-esteem after treason?

How to regain self-esteem if you cheated on your partner?

To begin with - stop practicing self-flagellation! If there was treason, it happened for a reason. Why did you do this? Perhaps the betrayal was committed against the background of a permanent misunderstanding of the partner, your needs were not fully met. Sometimes incidents happen - we do what we do. In a sense, the work of a psychotherapist brings undoubted advantages - certain situations are perceived more calmly, and the ability to stop self-flagellation and not incur ruthless criticism increases. Moreover, as practice shows, supervision helps to accept and admit one's mistakes, and when doing "work on mistakes", a person will do different things in the future.

My personal opinion about treason - I do not see anything reprehensible in this. It's bad if the partner finds out about this - it means that the person unconsciously (but on purpose!) Wanted this to happen, trying to show something to his loved one. It was probably difficult to say directly about the problems, or the partner did not want to listen to the arguments. Think of cheating as a crisis in your relationship.

There is also a negative point - according to statistics, after the betrayal, the couples do not stay together (and even more so if the partner finds out about the betrayal!). There are reverse situations - partners continue the relationship.

Forgive betrayal or not? This is another question. Metaphorically, treason can be compared to an "explosion of abscess" - a large inflamed purulent pimple gradually matures on the face ... and puff! There was a betrayal, and he burst. In other words, one of the partners could not tolerate discontent, irritation and dissatisfaction with the other. It is important to understand here that society and moral standards exert severe psychological pressure on us ("Treason! How terrible and unacceptable!"). Indeed, the situation is unpleasant, but vital - many people live like this.

There are couples in which both partners "walk", or they agree ("Live as you want, and I will live like that, too, but let's keep the relationship and sometimes make love").

In fact, in their understanding, one does not cancel the other; accordingly, relations are maintained. Lovers are a destructive stabilizer of families, so it is likely that after a betrayal, family relationships will change for the better. In most cases, this happens if the partner did not know about the betrayal. Otherwise, you will have to talk a lot on this topic. Some people are very careful and jealous of a sense of fidelity - in such situations it is important for them to receive a promise that this will not happen again ("That's all, it will never happen again! I love and I can't live without you!"). Treason is a litmus test. It is at that moment when you commit treason that you will understand what exactly you want - to stay with a partner or to leave.

Quite often, the cheater does not go to the lover, but to the void. Why it happens? The thing is that a person does not feel anything (guilt here is not taken into account). Let me give you an example from practice - a woman with an insane sense of guilt committed treason, not realizing to the end that she was not specifically comfortable with her partner, but realizing that there would be no further relationship.

As a result, for five years she could not find a partner, naively believing that she was "overtaken by karma" for perfect treason. There is no karma! In this case, karma is your own fault in relation to yourself, and your soul for some reason just needed a similar experience.

So, turn off all emotions and soberly analyze the situation -

Why did I do this?
What am I missing in a relationship?
What would you like to receive more from your partner?
What gave me such a lover / lover, unlike a wife / husband?

Why are lovers considered to be a destructive stabilizer of the family? Even the most unsatisfied partner in the relationship, "going to the side", compensates for everything that he lacked in the relationship.

Accordingly, he returns home happy, so he will be able to endure the current situation with his partner.

Perhaps, having changed, you hoped that it would become easier for you, you will understand your true needs, or you were trying to find a partner with common values. Treason is not the end of the world, and there really is nothing wrong with that! Today we are surrounded by a world of open doors and opportunities. Everyone is free to do what he wants, and considering that he has made a mistake, everyone has the right to apologize and receive forgiveness.

Treason is the same crisis as another turning point in life. If this event happened in your life, you need to figure out why you did this.

Further - no accusations and self-criticism. Work on the reasons, satisfy your needs in some way, so that in the future you do not "eat yourself from the inside", tormented by feelings of guilt.

It's better to turn off your guilty feelings, otherwise sooner or later it will catch up and become a cause of self-flagellation and destructive behavior - as a result, trying to punish yourself, you will not be able to be in a relationship or you will unconsciously look for a partner who will hurt.

How to get rid of love addiction?

You lost yourself in your loved one, you are drawn to him with some incredible, even inhuman, power. You grab onto the phone, rushing to write him an SMS, then yank yourself, delete the draft message, close and postpone the phone ... Another half hour later, and you reach for the phone again. You really want someone to break your hands or scold you, if only you would not write. You understand that you are already annoying him, he cannot stand you, but, alas ... you can't do anything with yourself. Such behavior can be observed both on the part of the man and on the part of the woman - a kind of love addiction.

To begin with, do not take all further words as an appeal "Run and get faster!". You need to run in very extreme cases, when unhealthy symptoms in a relationship manifest themselves stably. However, in most cases, it is quite possible to cope with love, even if your loved one has made the opposite decision.

Why is that? Newton's second law also applies to psychology. The more you apply force of action, the greater will be the force of reaction. And even if the partner treats you well and loves, in response to your behavior he will turn on the strength of resistance. How to get rid of love addiction? To start, stop doing something, stop! The next step is the most difficult.

Turn to yourself, look deep into your consciousness and try to understand what exactly is happening to you. When you understand this, it will become much easier for you.

Realize the true root of the problem - you have an affection trauma that is related to the mother figure. As a rule, people with such a problem, neurotic, may even be in the border zone of the organization of the psyche. These are individuals who had a violation in the zone of merging or separation with the mother's object of attachment (hyper-custody mother, grandmother, grandfather, but at the same time these people were completely not emotionally involved in the upbringing - they did not pay attention to the desires and needs of the child, preferring that he blindly fulfilled their requirements).

But most importantly, no one emotionally invested in the child, they treated him rather coldly (even if someone was nearby 24/7, the baby did not feel real care, attention and warmth). Quite often, maternal figures are "frozen" mothers who lost a baby before you were born and could not cope with this loss, hard-working mothers who work all day at work, anxious mothers who constantly find out relationships with their father or other men (emotionally, they cared about everything anything but your own child).

There may be a slightly different situation - because of your own guilt, your mother was more involved in her relationship with her grandmother, she paid special attention to her, constantly worrying that she would be offended (grandmother would be offended - you need to visit her, call, do what she wants). If we consider the hierarchy according to Bert Hellinger (our parents are behind, and we are moving forward in our future), such relationships are reversed. In other words, the whole flow of mother's love goes around you. As a result, against this background, a person develops a neurosis, and then he unconsciously (but on purpose!) Searches for a person with whom he can play this scenario again. For what? To show himself that he can change the situation, he can change himself, and the flow of love this time will not bypass him. In the video "The Mechanism of Love Dependence", a separate stage is singled out at which a person begins to bother his partner strongly in various ways - jealousy, suspicions, frequent calls and messages, annoying requests. At some point in your life, you became a lot for your partner, and he began to fence himself off. As a rule, a person who tends to fall into love addiction will do everything to bother a partner, and then deal with it. For him, this is a kind of passion, an incomparable adrenaline and drug - a thrill of rather painful suffering, a sea of tears, burning unspoken insults ... However, the psyche continues to demand: "Give me a man for whom I must fight!" That is why you need to carefully understand your personal situation inside your consciousness (For whom are you fighting like that? Who did not give you the love and care that you so wanted to receive?). Why is this necessary? You do not need to project what you have experienced before, you should realize that mom is a mother's figure, and a man or woman is another person.

Seeing the difference, you can act differently, however, you need to consider that new neural connections are formed for a long time. Ideally, psychotherapy sessions are needed here, because you yourself will not be able to understand at what stage you re-entered into a vicious circle with the next person. Alas, however much we would like to quickly solve the problem, even therapy will not help. What is the danger of constant love affection? You are exhausting yourself, and in the end you will cease to believe the whole world, and you will cease to perceive love as a pure and sincere feeling. There are situations when love affection leads to severe depression, suicide, murder of a beloved partner. Work on yourself and your feelings in order not to reach the "bottom of life". So, how to get out of the state of love addiction?

Before you apply any of the following techniques, you need to:

Set a clear goal - to get rid of love addiction, no matter what. This decision must be strong-willed, tough and persistent, no need to cancel it.

Use all possible support resources that you find. Understanding that breaking a relationship is not necessary. However, as a rule, the psyche will demand satisfaction - as a child, you could not break the connection with the maternal object, separation from the parent did not occur.

So why not break this vicious circle right now? Techniques for developing love addiction Deidealization. In the case of love, we idealize in the relationship of our partner. Its advantages seem invaluable, and we do not see a flaw at all.

Take 2 blank sheets of paper and a pen (you can use a laptop). First write on all the advantages of a loved one (so you slightly reduce the resistance), on the second - the disadvantages. Opposite each advantage, indicate why you "came up with" it, that is, "translate" it into a disadvantage (for example, a partner is rather economical, but in fact he can be mean or greedy). Then reinforce the flaws. If you have not found at least 5 shortcomings of a partner, you have not made a tough decision to say goodbye to love addiction, you are comfortable and like to be in this state - suffer further! This technique should be applied immediately after the first. Imagine that your relationship has developed normally - What will it be like in a year, two, five? How will all household issues affect this? Try not to think about "butterflies in the stomach" ("Oh, it will be so wonderful to cook breakfast for him in the morning, collect his socks all over the apartment and wash. I would wash his socks every 5 minutes!"), Soberly assess the situation without romantic pathos . Imagine that for 5 years now every day you see this person next to you. Now you know him far and wide, he tells the same stories and tales, makes the same mistakes, he is also late for your dates, does not answer phone calls, thinks only of his beloved, does not take out the trash, etc. .

Transfer all negative everyday moments that have ever occurred in your life (in any relationship) to the current situation and imagine that it will be so. Over time, any couple is faced with deep domestic problems and monotony in relationships.

In general, all healthy relationships are rather boring (there is no whole life of romantic pathos and a candy-bouquet period). To all this, imagine how all the shortcomings of the partner are manifested, exaggerate much of each of them. So, the second technique according to Sigmund Freud. It is quite simple - sublimate. In other words, relieve internal stress by redirecting energy toward more acceptable goals. Remember what you love to do (sing, dance, draw, write poetry, make music, etc.), and do it! You will not only get rid of love addiction, but also discover a new hobby. It is better to do some kind of creativity - so you can fully immerse yourself in a new business, and everything else will recede into the background. Put an empty chair in front of you and tell him everything that you would like to tell your partner. This is a technique from gestalt therapy. This can be all the accumulated anger (for all wrong actions or inaction), an apology (maybe you didn't do something for your partner). Understand that lost love is not the only painful factor. It hurts you and the fact that you could not give your partner love in return, did not direct the flow of love in the way you would like it to. Try to forgive yourself for what you could not do, have made many mistakes in life (now you understand and know them). Remember to thank - this is an important point.

Be sure to find something to thank the person for (even if it will be some kind of trifle) and try to let go of him. This is the most difficult step to take to get rid of love addiction. Remember that love is primarily a concern for another person, so forget about your own pain and personal needs. If the other person wants to see you less often, this is his right, and your permission is absolutely not necessary for this.

Give yourself the right to accept the situation in general. Relatively speaking, you can do this through pain and suffering or more gently.

Give yourself time (a week, two, a month) to mourn the pathological relationship for you and your partner, consider what exactly did not work out and why. Release the hopes associated with your loved one ("Yes, everything would be wonderful ... But ... Not with him!"). If you still managed to maintain a relationship, act peacefully: - Having experienced all the shortcomings of a partner, imagine how you will continue to build relationships (in 5 years); - Think about how they will look after everything that you have expressed to a person (in this case, an empty chair).

Further continue to communicate with your partner as if nothing had happened. In fact, inside your consciousness you no longer perceive it as an ideal and do not despise all the shortcomings - metaphorically, your attitude to your loved one is on the balanced scale. Why? You have experienced all the pain from his loss inside the subconscious, reconciled to the fact that at any moment he can leave, and you have to let go. If you did everything right, were honest with yourself, the turbulent energy flow between you is harmonized.

Our lives and emotions are structured in such a way that at some point we can again find ourselves in this vicious circle. In this case, repeat all the exercises again - deidealization, sublimation and the "empty chair" technique. Your task is to reach the "0" mark in relation to the partner inside your mind and it's easier to react further to everything that happens. An important point - even if you did everything right, worked through each exercise, you do not need to rush to call or write to a person again.

Do not think that now everything will be different. This will happen again and you will again be addicted to your loved one! Love dependence can be compared with a rushing train at a speed of 330 km / h. You need to stop it - through tears, living grief, farewell to a partner, humility, bitter disappointment.

So, we work with our consciousness and go to the "0" position, and only then we begin to act as if there was no love dependence. If this is not the first situation for you, find the strength in yourself to carefully analyze it - that means your life wants to show something.

How to deal with procrastination?

Procrastination is a tendency to constantly postpone things "for later" (including important and urgent ones!). This condition becomes a real problem when a person is in it most of the time - constant "breakdowns" of planned affairs, poor-quality result and, as a result, stress, guilt, troubles and missed opportunities.

In fact, procrastination is a very slow but sure way to reach the edge of life. Why do you need to fight procrastination, and how to do it?

What is the essence of procrastination?

A person neglects specific important matters and is distracted by various trifles and entertainments. For example, to skip classes at the institute and make a website at home, the purpose of which is still not even clearly understood; Do not go to work and do house cleaning; do not record an important video and wash dishes, etc. Each person tends to procrastinate in one way or another - even the most successful one! However, creative personalities suffer the most from this psychological phenomenon - it is often the aesthetes of the beautiful who sit at home for days and only by three o'clock do they begin to do some work. What is the basis of the phenomenon of procrastination? Fear of luck and victory, a feeling of fear of getting really tangible results (as a rule, procrastination occurs at those times when a person has a very high motivation). Fear of something new - you don't know what to do, so there is an alarming feeling of "meeting a tiger." Fear of disgrace in front of other people. Fear of doing stupid things and making a mistake - all of a sudden I won't succeed; the result will be much worse than other people; do not meet my expectations? Fear of shame accompanies many of us (it doesn't matter if you have the makings of a perfectionist or not).

Lack of support and, as a result, lack of internal resources (you don't have energy, or it is simply spent on fighting an oppressive sense of fear to be ashamed and not get moral support from loved ones).

You are trying to find information on how to do this, or you don't even know where to start - a lot of energy is spent on all this. And even doing household chores (for example, cleaning the kitchen or washing dishes), you nevertheless spend your internal resources in double volume - and for the important work that you did not do and set aside "for later".

Thus, an overspending of energy is obtained. In addition, you may be disturbed by a state of depression, increased anxiety, apathy and bad mood, high expectations (for example, my mother said that I should be the best, and my grandmother expected only good results - "five" in all subjects). In the latter case, often no one praises the child and is not happy with good grades (everything is limited to the standard phrase - "Yes, that's right!"), Parents react only to "fours" and "triples". As a result, a person has the beginnings of a procrastinating character. Why it happens?

If you notice a person only in moments of failure, you will unconsciously provoke a similar behavior so that you are noticed when you are at the very bottom ("Oh, good! I need to go down even lower and relatives will notice me - mom, dad, husband ... "). Relatively speaking, you broadcast to others: "Look at me, what a poor thing I am! I can't do anything, I don't have the strength and energy ... Drag me seven, I myself can't! "). The habit of having instant pleasure.

In practice, it looks like this - you merge the accumulated energy and tension into petty household chores, "deceiving" your psyche ("Look, I'm doing an important thing - washing my dishes, cleaning my apartment, reading a book. I'm not sitting still!") .

As a result, the tension goes away, and the person gives himself a promise to do the "thing" later. What happens next? Everything postponed "for later" is forgotten, this happens regularly, and a person simply degrades, does not think strategically and, accordingly, does not take a single step in the direction of his success, in fact he takes the position of the enemy of any undertakings and attempts. How to get rid of procrastination? Sooner or later, you will avoid important and priority tasks and this will lead to the fact that things will accumulate exponentially, and it will become difficult for you to force yourself to do them over time.

It is understandable that you will resist the fulfillment of the accumulated tasks. What do we have as a result? In the worst case scenario, you suddenly find yourself on the edge of life without work and money. What to do? To begin with, you should catch yourself at the moment when you procrastinate and say: "Enough! I don't want to bring myself to the very extreme state of degradation! "

Ask yourself what might happen if you do not change your behavior. Are you comfortable with life now? And what will happen if it remains so - is that the norm for you? If you answered "yes", then there is no point in reading - return to your usual environment and go further downstream. However, as a rule, we all strive for development, this is due to our nature. If you strongly disagree with the current state of affairs in your life, begin to catch yourself at the moments of procrastination. For example, you have now decided to wash the dishes, but why do not you want to do a more urgent and important task? What are you afraid of? Shame, failure, defeat, condemnation of others, or maybe you don't even know where to start?

Give yourself a specific answer. Answer the following questions: - Do you have enough knowledge? - What kind of knowledge do you lack? "Do you have enough energy?" Where can you get the energy you need to move forward? - Do you have enough support? Where can you find her?

Try to apply a rather interesting psychological technique - imagine that your undertaking is successful (for example, you successfully recorded a video and millions of subscribers started to watch you). What emotions do you get? Will you gain recognition, or envy will surround you, your family will renounce you (relatives prefer and support only the poor, and those who succeed are treated with contempt and silent condemnation)?

Carefully analyze the answers to these questions.

Think and remember for what actions in childhood you were loved, and for which you experienced complete indifference. The phenomenon of procrastination is closely interconnected with the indifference of relatives and close people - most of all in life you are afraid to find yourself in a situation where you will be indifferent. For example, no one praised you for a beautiful drawing, but did not punish you, your family reacted to this apathetic and indifferent. As a result, a person stops at the place of receiving some really effective and important skills in life.

Be sure to write down all the reasons that could affect your current condition.

Be honest with yourself, go to the depths of your soul, early childhood and the very first childhood experiences, honestly answer the question what exactly are you afraid of in a particular situation, what are you missing, what is the true reason for procrastination.

So, you figured out the real nature of your procrastination. Now confront yourself.

Clearly and clearly make it clear to your consciousness that the responsibility for your life lies only with you. Nobody will fulfill your tasks for you and live your life, and most importantly - just because no one will give you anything! At a minimum, you will pay with suffering, worries, attention, or even psychological trauma.

Make a to-do list for every day. If you find it difficult to start doing something, add this unwanted business to it every day. It is important to identify the most important task. If it's impossible and difficult for you now, break it down into sub-tasks, indicate specific steps to achieve the desired goal — only so that you will probably begin to carry it out today. Let it be just a small step - it doesn't matter! Use the Pomodoro method - 25/5 (25 minutes you work, 5 minutes rest). Do not drive yourself into work, let rest and relax, gather your thoughts. Otherwise, you simply won't believe yourself, when once again you start working, you will certainly understand that you won't be able to rest in the next three hours.

We put rational restrictions in the workflow! Use affirmations. It is a simple verbal formula written in a positive way that will allow you to fix the desired attitude in your subconscious mind ("I will succeed," "I will find an additional resource," "I have something to work for").

If you constantly scroll through affirmations in your head or record them on a voice recorder, this will help you overcome mental resistance.

How to overcome laziness?

What are the causes of laziness? How to deal with this pathological inaction?

In fact, laziness can be divided into two problems - the problem with motivation and the problem with willpower. So what are the main causes of laziness in relation to motivation?

Not strong enough motivation. Relatively speaking, if in the evening I need to get out of the couch in order to earn some 100 dollars, which absolutely do not make any weather in the house, I will hardly get out of the couch. Really, why?

100 dollars more, 100 dollars less ... If it was about 10,000 dollars, I would immediately jump out of bed and run to do something. Sometimes there is a slightly different situation - you do not fully understand what the result will

be. In this case, motivation is not motivation. You do not really believe that you will get a tangible result, do not give yourself that right. In fact, faith is simply giving yourself the right ("I have the right to earn these 10 thousand dollars in half an hour, which means I will get up and do it!"). If I do not give myself such a right, no matter how I get up and try to complete the task, I will not succeed. Accordingly, all this refers to not too strong motivation and goal.

Motivation and goal always follow in parallel with each other. What is the difference between these two concepts? The goal implies a specific task, for example, to earn $ 100 in half an hour and then regularly earn that amount.

Motivation may mean that I will not get the result right now, and it will not be in specific numbers, but that I will become better, develop, etc.

Thus, motivation is a process, a goal is a result. If a person's goal is too high (he does not believe that he can achieve certain results; he does not know what kind of efforts he should make for this), this will slow down his motivation. Metaphorically, motivation can be compared to the energy that pulls us forward towards the goal. Purpose and needs do not match. The goal is a clear task with deadlines and amounts ("I want to consistently earn 10 thousand dollars a month!").

Motivation is what motivates you to earn these 10 thousand dollars a month. So, you want to earn or receive a specific amount, but your body resists ("What will I do with this money? I don't need expensive branded clothes, I don't need to pay a mortgage for an apartment ... You can buy a car with this money, but why ? "), The energy inside you does not turn on (" Well, fine, but no! "). And whatever you offer yourself, consciousness does not respond to the call.

It's quite a common occurrence when people say that they want to earn a lot, but when they see a couple in love, they have tears in their eyes, their hearts tremble in their chests - inside the mind, the reaction goes to completely different things. This is a kind of substitution - I want to earn a lot, but in reality I want to love and be in harmonious and beautiful relationships like everyone else.

There is a reverse situation - a person tries in every possible way to deal with family relationships, but in fact is worried about debts and payment to contractors, is looking for additional ways to earn money to invest in business. The body gives him a hint that real interest is not in relationships, but in money. And until this basic spiritual need is settled, it will be impossible to solve other problems. Where human interest is concentrated, there will be more energy, respectively, and these tasks will be solved with greater efficiency.

An abstract goal (no specific desires, no concrete visualization, no clear understanding of what exactly you want). It may be that there are thoughts, but your soul does not agree to follow this path, therefore the goal remains at the level of the abstract task (you do not see and feel it). When a person sees a conscious and understandable goal in front of him, he seems to feel it, it is practically in his hands. Then the energy is turned on. An internal resource is not connected to an abstract target; in fact, it does not exist. If you don't know what exactly you want to achieve (I want - I don't want to), then you don't want this at all. Conclusion - this will not be motivation, you will continue to be lazy, because the energy has not risen.

The most important point of all three points - pure desire and energy should be stronger than all your beliefs, attitudes, ideas, goals. It should "pull" you from the inside. If this is not the case, once again you will lie limp on the bed and watch the series for the twenty-fifth time - it's all the same what to do, just to not do that thing! How to deal with insufficient motivation and what to do with all this? Set clear, concise, and understandable goals.

 First of all, identify the basic need, for this, turn to the deepest part of your soul, which really knows what it needs most. No matter how you deceive yourself ("I need to earn more!"), If your soul wants peace and relaxation, the arms of a loved one, tender, romantic and pleasant dates, you will not succeed in the material sphere.

Recognize this need! Naturally, there are situations when a conflict arises and grows inside the mind - you may want to cuddle with your loved one for days, but you still need to earn money, because after some time you will want to eat. In this case, everything will be the way you agree with your inner child.

Sit down, look inside your consciousness, pay attention to your needs, acknowledge them and tell yourself: "Yes, I see, feel, hear, understand that you now want more hugs, love and romance, but there is another more important task. If we do not fulfill it, we will not have ice cream, sweets, a new dress. We will not pay for utilities, we will not buy delicious food, etc. " Say what is important for you in this zone and agree with yourself: "Look, today we will take a walk, but then we will work for two days." In any conflict, the main thing is to find a compromise, so find this balance within your mind.

In the case of the opposite situation (you tell yourself that you need to understand the relationship, and money is hovering at the very same place), agree again: "Well, let me postpone this issue now, I'll agree with my wife. I understand that we have a protracted serious conflict, this crisis needs to be resolved, but right now my project is on fire, I need to do this. Let's you and I raise this issue in a week, but for now we'll live without emotions, just try to turn them off. "

If we consider the deeper reasons that influenced the fact that your motivation stopped "turning on" and you began to "push" it into yourself, you can distinguish overwhelming parents and relatives who pushed any strong excitement back. Accordingly, you have become accustomed from a very early age to a situation where when you were happy, your mom, dad, grandfather or grandmother simply "pushed" it back into your mind ("Why are you jumping on the bed? Sit and sit, don't! Now you will fall!") . Relatively speaking, you were forced to play a quiet game, and this is tantamount to punishment, because you wanted to throw out a full charge of energy. If in childhood you had similar situations, the worked-out mechanism has already been fixed in the subconscious. As soon as the excitement comes, something inspires you greatly, you pull yourself - sit still, you can't do anything, because you are not worth it; you cannot receive what your arousal wants; you have to sit quietly in the corner and do not want anything in this life.

Thus, you "wrap yourself in", and after that you don't want anything. What you really wanted to receive in life, you cannot; you yourself convinced yourself that wanting something badly - it hurts.

Conclusion - I will not do this, it's better I will pretend that I do not want anything. So a person suppresses in himself any energy, excitement and inspiration - he was already taught to do it successfully in childhood.

Learn to include your desires, begin to listen to them, find out your true needs, no matter how painful it is! The situation when a person chooses between relationships and money is quite common in our time. Against this background, many people are changing - I want a relationship, but I'm going to get a second job. Why? It is painful for a person to recognize the fact that he really wants simple human attention, emotional inclusion, care and relationships - simple things that were supplanted for him in childhood were rejected by family members (they could even be ashamed of the need for emotional contact).

So, if the family has frozen the need of the child, in adulthood he will have a rather painful perception of his true need, and, as a result, the substitution will begin.
The next stage is laziness and procrastination. Look for your basic need, then you can find the internal energy for its implementation. And energy is the motivation that will carry you to your goal. Only then will laziness disappear!

How to develop willpower?

How does the problem of willpower affect laziness?

To begin with, let's figure out what may lie at the heart of laziness. Depression. A depressed and depressed mental state, when pessimism rolls over, a person can experience as laziness. However, in reality this is not a lack of desire to do anything, but very serious hormonal disorders that cannot be corrected by the power of thought alone.

If you are in a state of severe clinical depression, consult a psychiatrist for a course of treatment. In this case, working with willpower will not give positive results, on the contrary - you can bring yourself almost to suicide. Why?

Depression is a mental disorder characterized by depressed mood, loss of strength, fatigue and loss of interest in everything. Starting with seemingly simple symptoms of sleep disturbance and poor appetite, this condition quickly becomes a cause of interruptions with neurotransmitters, blocks the synthesis of serotonin and dopamine, over time you will be visited more often by bad thoughts, overcome laziness and unwillingness to do anything, apathy will awaken and lethargy.

Syndrome of learned helplessness. This condition is rooted in childhood - mother, father, brother, sister always did everything for you (up to lacing shoes!). Often, it is for younger children in the family that laziness and procrastination are characteristic. There can be two options: - a large family, respectively, a lot of older people - everyone is in a hurry somewhere, so the child was quickly combed, dressed, fastened; - one hyper-custody mother - the child has not even had time to want something, as everyone has already given him (for example, he said that he wants to eat - a three-course table was immediately laid, etc.).

So, a person from childhood was not taught to strain in order to get what he wanted.

In fact, today it is the biggest problem. Many young people do not want to strain and are outraged that they do not succeed, there are no tangible results in life. From the side it seems that "their muscles simply atrophied." What to do?

Treat depression if you still have it. If you do not suffer from depressive disorder, make a tough and strong-willed decision that you will work with your willpower and strive to become stronger (relatively speaking, "pump up" the willpower muscle). If there are no newly revealed circumstances or situations, or the general situation has not changed much, do not deviate from the plan. Begin to "pull out" bit by bit all those desires that you have.

As a child, you didn't have time to want something, but everything was already served to you on a silver platter, so now it's important for you to gradually draw out your true desires from consciousness, and not the desires and expectations of mom, dad, grandmother. Quite often, men try to please their parents. For example, the father lives in the world of material values, he has money, status and position in the first place, and his son is a creative person (wants to draw or dance). As a rule, in this situation, the child will either never be able to please the dad and receive, accordingly, the satisfaction of the boy; or never satisfy himself.

If we consider both situations from a psychological point of view, the second is much worse - having received status, money and other privileges ("Dad, look how good I am! I achieved everything you wanted!"), The man will feel that he has not realized himself as a person and lost a part of himself somewhere on the road to fulfilling the wishes of the parent.

Remember your childhood dreams, start with little things - what do you want to eat, where to go, what to see, what to do? Try to fulfill long-forgotten desires. For example, you use a certain type of pen, but to buy one, you have to go two more quarters, and even after work. In this case, if you do not make a firm decision and do not focus on it, you will be lazy for at least a few days. You need to do the opposite - I wanted to buy a pen, get up and go buy it.

There are situations when a desire can be delayed, but it must be satisfied sooner or later. Let your psyche understand that you have a desire, a goal, an intention to achieve it and get satisfaction from the result. In fact, you should get much more satisfaction from the result than from resistance to this action now. For example, you have decided to tighten your figure and go to the gym, but not today ("It's better to eat a burger!").

Your psyche in this situation receives instant satisfaction (you tensed up, because you need to go to the gym, and immediately relaxed - it will not be today!). Having made a firm decision to visit the gym, you experience prolonged stress (to pack, get dressed, take a bag with replaceable clothes, work out the entire lesson (2-3 hours), return home, take a shower, etc. However, when you see the result on the scales and in the mirror, this inner satisfaction is difficult to compare with instant pleasure - it is felt inside your consciousness as a life-giving force.

Do not forget to praise yourself for achievements. Forming this power in this way every time, you will gradually grow above yourself. So, you have there is a desire - strive to fulfill it. It doesn't matter how long this process takes - do it! This way you show that you are a confident person, a strong personality who can take his destiny and himself in hands, change habits. Write a list of habits, which you would like to introduce into your life. Try to introduce one habit a month, for example, get up every day and do exercises in the morning or fill out a diary in the evening emotions.

Moving step by step, you will strengthen your willpower and self-esteem at the same time. And then laziness will gradually recede, and your "muscle of tension" will be trained. Anyone who visits the gym for more than 2-3 years, feels a wild delight from the training process itself. The same thing happens in any other area.

The most important thing is to give a gradual load, otherwise the body will resist, and you will not want to have a beautiful figure, complete a new project or wake up in a good mood.

How to overcome shame?

Why are we afraid to experience this feeling and avoid it in every way? And what can this lead to in the end?

To some extent, this is an escape from all situations that can cause shame - the fear of being humiliated, the fear of getting criticism in one's direction. In this case, criticism is perceived not through guilt (I did something wrong!), But through the humiliation of my actions (I'm a bad person, because I'm doing something bad!). This is an early and very deep mental disorder, not psychosis, not a disorder, but a deep problem, on the basis of which self-esteem decreases and it is difficult to build any kind of relationship.

A person who is afraid to feel shame is a person who avoids any publicity and relationships in general, it is difficult for her to visit crowded places, to show herself in society ("God forbid, I will do something wrong! I'm bad and everyone will notice it! "). A great example is the protagonist from the movie Jumanji: A New Level. When the girl invited him to talk frankly and find out why they could not be together, the guy replied: "If you saw who I really am … After all, I'm completely different from that in this space! You would definitely leave me! " In response, the girl said: "Yes, I also have such a difficulty. I'm afraid that everyone will see me for who I am.

That is why we avoid relationships. But the most important thing is that when I look at you, I feel good! The rest simply does not matter. " Why do such people avoid relationships? Not even because others will notice them! The thing is that they themselves are afraid to notice in themselves what will make them feel shame. And the feeling of shame and embarrassment is so all-consuming, squeezing our body from the inside, that we often close ourselves in ourselves, as if hiding in a shell (like turtles) - everything, don't look at me, I'm very ashamed and uncomfortable that you noticed me!

By and large, a person's intolerance to shame is of great importance. It is common for all of us to experience this feeling for one or another action, to be embarrassed and feel awkward, and here it is so unbearable that we are fencing ourselves off from the whole world and closing ourselves ("I know for sure that I am a bad person! And they will all see! And I for I'll emphasize myself again this unpleasant fact ").

A separate type of fear of shame is the fear of authorities (the fear of people who occupy a vertical position - this may be the oldest person on whom you are addicted). In this situation, spontaneous self-expression, unexpected actions are also blocked (in other words, you are not able to live your life without thinking about anything - "I want to play, have fun and generally say what I want!"). Because of the authority before you, you immediately decrease, becoming small. What are the causes of fear of shame?

If it is connected with the fear of authorities, the leading role in the formation of this sensation was played by parental figures (mom, dad, or all those who raised the child) who always tried to suppress children's energy of excitement ("Do not jump on the couch! Sit quietly!", "Do not act like that, better shut up! "," You broke a mug, how bad you are! "etc.). The ego is formed at an early age (from a year to three years), then shame is also formed. In general, as a social feeling, shame is quite acceptable and has a positive character - this is how you can rethink your behavior ("Did I really behave badly? What was wrong?").

If a person addressed the audience, received negative feedback, you need to rethink your actions when you return home ("What was wrong with my speech? How can I improve it?"). However, often the feeling of shame completely unsettles us, falling like a tsunami, and stunned, we are not able to do anything. Why?

Getting into your childhood experiences (you just started walking and exploring the world around you, ruined your mother's lipstick, painted wallpapers, etc.) when mom, dad, grandfather or grandfather stood over us with his hands on our sides: "What have you done ?!" , a person perceives the situation as a whole as if no one loves him ("I'm bad and nobody needs me!").

In fact, the desire to pick up something, turn it around, touch it, etc. - this is idovskaya energy, so stormy and uncontrollable that it does not need to be explained in any way (I want it!). There is a contradiction - I want to, but it is not approved by anyone, even condemned, which means - I'm bad! As a result, in adulthood, a person closes any excitement with shame: "No, I can't want something!

You cannot manifest how I want.

You can't do spontaneous acts ... "

As a rule, if the degree of conviction was quite high, you cannot allow yourself to manifest in anything. Another reason is a close relative raising a child (mom, grandmother, dad or grandfather - someone who had a strong emotional contact with the child) was himself a rather bashful person (in the foreground there was always a question - what would the neighbors think?).

Accordingly, the child absorbs the shame of the parent, like a sponge, and in the future will reproduce it as a shameful person, fearing the manifestation of this feeling and each time falling into the ground, because it is unbearable! What to do with all this?

1. "Shame" yourself a little bit - allow yourself to get into awkward situations when you let others know that they are not ideal. At the same time, be sure to find yourself an excuse every time, analyze the overall situation and think over actions for the future.

Why is it difficult for some people to use this technique? Getting into a shameful situation, you are hiding from everyone (everything, I'm in the house!). This is a kind of child protection - "I do not see, which means that this is not!" (pure negation). And you will not look at the real reaction of others to your action.

2. Group psychotherapy - you can see that not only are you ashamed of some nonsense, other people are also worried! At first, I was always interested in acquaintances, and even colleagues, whether my statements were so terrible, and when I received feedback, I calmed down.

Look realistically in the eye! Do not be afraid of the response of others. Even if they tell you that you have "gone too far", this will be a lesson for the future, you will be able to evaluate your behavior from the outside and next time act differently.

Be sure to work on your fear, fall into shame, but come back.

To get into the funnel of shame is normal, the main thing is to analyze the reactions of real people, because nobody stops loving us because we crap one's pants!

How to drive a woman crazy in 2 minutes?

How to please a woman, make a pleasant first impression?

The main criterion is that a man should give the impression of a confident person, feel like a winner, radiate inner strength. All this can manifest itself in behavior, eyes, movements, but the most important thing is that inside a person really feels that way and manifests accordingly.

Why is this criterion paramount?

All people are biological creatures, everyone has instincts, one of which can be equated with the survival instinct - this is the instinct of reproduction. Each of us wants our generation to be strong and strong, able to survive in the changing environment. And what is the main role a man plays in relation to a woman? Security, protection, stability, confidence that everything will be - in other words, helps to survive. Especially when a woman is on maternity leave and nurses the baby for the first year, it is very important that the man can confidently lead his family by the hand through life.

Money is not a fundamental factor in choosing a man. According to statistics, for only 10-20% of women it is important that the satellite earn a lot. This topic really matters a lot, but the projection of a man is more likely tied up here. Relatively speaking, you would also like for someone to take responsibility and provide for you. Such a desire is quite normal - none of us is deprived of childhood illusory dreams that now someone will appear and save us. Another thing - how do we deal with this?

Men are much easier to drive crazy than women, and this factor is directly related to the difference in biology. At least in the weaker sex, the orgasmic center is located in more than one part of the brain, unlike men.

So, it's quite difficult to instantly drive a woman crazy, you need to perform a series of actions - show respect, pay attention, take care of her - do everything that will make her first impression and give her firm confidence. Show the woman that you are the very male who will definitely survive in wildlife, protect her and her offspring from some worldly troubles, and this is absolutely not necessary to do with money. You can earn little money, provide for yourself and your family, protect against those who attack and want to destroy the family hearth, take care (meet in the evenings, etc.).

Courage can also be attributed to confidence - a brave and confident man will always be between a woman and a potentially dangerous person, trying to protect her.

Another important point - you should not have any psychological barriers in terms of fears, shame and guilt, which can block you from contact. If so, then self-confidence will be even stronger, stronger and will be broadcast to all the females surrounding you. And do not torment yourself - even if you are not a $ 100 bill, everyone doesn't like it, there is a woman who considers your calm confidence and poise and will definitely join her, wants to be with you. If you think that you, besides confidence, have nothing else - that's already a lot! And a woman with a healthy psyche will see and appreciate it!

Develop this quality in your mind, then outwardly you will be attractive to any rational woman!

How to prevent treason?

In any relationship, betraying a partner is his responsibility and decision (the person has decided so, which means he needed it that way). Sometimes, no matter how one of the partners tries to make the relationship perfect, the second one still looks to the left ("like he doesn't feed the wolf, he looks into the forest"). How to prevent treason? What needs to be done so that the partner feels good next to you?

1. Let's start "from the opposite." What can not be done in any case? Do not punish your partner for lack of sex or emotional cold. Often, almost all parents behave in a similar way, when the children are small - they use the method of "emotional estrangement" if the child is coddling and not listening. We carry this line of behavior into adulthood, which as a result leads to a completely justified reaction from the partner ("Well, since you are so angry and unbalanced, I will find a more kind woman"). Nowadays, both men and women are punished by sex, but punishment by the absence of sexual relations is akin to childish behavior. Learn to communicate with a partner, you don't need to sit in different corners of the room and wait until the other starts the conversation first ("Why are you offended (-is)?"). Try to overcome the resentment and clarify the situation so that there are no disagreements between you ("Let's talk. I don't think that the fault lies entirely with me, but it's important for me to discuss the situation with you so that resentment, anger, disappointment and frustration go by the wayside, and we could continue to live normally with you ").

2. Stop falling into paranoia. The more you try to "discover" a partner in something, show open distrust towards him, the more likely it can lead to

betrayal and betrayal. Such a simple axiom is due to the fact that one of the partners in the soul has an open trauma of rejection, treason, abandonment. Perhaps in childhood, he observed the betrayal of his parents and thus provokes another partner. Believe your loved one. Trust is a two-way road. You will trust the partner, he will trust in response. Paranoia most often occurs when partners move away from each other, against the background of a certain injury. A mental shock causes a certain tension, as a result one of the partners reacts sharply to the distance and the fact that the second has become emotionally cold, lingers longer at work, pays less attention to communication when he returns home, says little about himself, etc. As a result, emotional distrust, unreasonable suspicion is included. How to deal with this condition?

First you need to ask yourself: "What does not suit my partner in me? What does not satisfy? What could be the reason for his estrangement? " Perhaps you had too many in a relationship or, conversely, you ignored the partner's emotions at the moment when he needed care and emotional inclusion. " For example, after a year of joint relations, one of the partners had a life crisis, accordingly, a person wants to get more care and attention, and if he doesn't get what he wants, he will be offended ("You don't cook for me when I come home from work!", "You don't meet me ", etc.). As a rule, claims are voiced repeatedly, but the second partner does not pay attention to them, hoping that they will love him and accept him for who he is.

However, it is worth considering the downside - adult relationships by default assume a relationship. You give, they give you in return. That is why you should not ignore the wishes of your partner, listen to his needs, directly ask about what you like ("I noticed (a) that you have been moving away lately. What is this connected with?"). After receiving the answer, try to believe and hear exactly what the person wants to say, and not to imagine completely opposite scenes in the imagination.

3. Learn to forgive, close your eyes to some minor misconduct of your partner (an open tube of toothpaste, scattered hair, under-salted borsch, socks and shoes are not in place, etc.). How to do it? It is enough to analyze a simple situation. For example, a partner used a kitchen towel to wipe a table. If he focuses on this, firstly, he will no longer help in the kitchen, and secondly, the situation will cause a quarrel, resentment and, as a result, the partners will stop communicating. Is a towel worth arguing? Quite often we swear over trifles - we want it to be so, and that's it. But can this be put on the scale of your relationship?

4. In the relationship you need to add a "peppercorn" - not scandals, nit-picking and quarrels (although this depends on the couple, some, on the contrary, are screaming). On the Internet, you can find millions of tips on how to do this - eroticism, flirting, role-playing games in unusual clothes and an unexpected place.

The most important thing is the effect of surprise for the partner (an unusual romantic encounter, a completely new role in the relationship (a decent harlot girl), etc.).

5. Give each other a sense of significance and importance, show care, attention, respect and emotional warmth. Harmonious relationships are built on these whales. In fact, partners do not hold anything together except for emotional involvement in each other (admiration for each other, gleam in the eyes, some elusive excitement, a sense of significance, interest and involvement in the life of a loved one).

Communication with a psychotherapist is therefore valuable because, unlike many people in the world, a psychologist is fully committed to the client (all the emotions experienced are closely connected only with him). It was this kind of behavior that we lacked in childhood with our parents and we lack in adulthood in close relationships. If you can give it to your partner, he will never abandon you or change you.

How to increase self-esteem and stop being comfortable?

There is a certain category of people who are used to "being comfortable" with others, doing everything to make everyone around feel good, but at the same time they themselves suffer. How are self-esteem and desire to please everyone related?

So, how do you know a person who wants to be comfortable? He often praises others, appeases others, brings gifts and treats, agrees to fulfill any requests, never refuses anything, supports and finds the right words, always arrives at the request, that is, he will do everything to be as useful and necessary as possible for those around him. . Quite often, such people silently agree that they do not like and disgust their opinion ("Well, let it be as you say!"), Do not argue and do not share their personal opinions, flee to save someone, even if nobody asks for this. However, regardless of their good intentions and actions, they still remain depreciated, they do not like such people and do not perceive them in society (they do not give them as much love, attention and respect as they would like).

What is hidden under the "be comfortable" behavior for everyone? An inner need and an unconscious desire to be needed, which indicates that a person wants the approval and recognition of others (it is vital for him to be a good guy / girl, everyone must be proud of him, etc.). In fact, the more we cater to other people, the less they value and respect us. Why it happens? If a person asks for recognition, approval and respect from others, then he himself is not able to praise himself and be proud of his behavior. In addition, as a rule, such individuals lack the ability to accept respect and recognition, they even reject help ("No, thank you! I will figure it out myself," "No need, why should I?"). As a result, a serious psychological imbalance is formed - the need is high ("Give me this, please! I really want to be appreciated!"), But as soon as a person is given what he wants, he nullifies everything inside his mind. With each situation, the gap between need and psyche widens. All this is experienced by a person inside, and directly in dealing with such a person a feeling of pity may arise ("Poor thing! He distributes everything to everyone, but he doesn't take anything in return!") And disrespect. What is the way out of the situation?
1. Put in the first place their values, desires and unwillingness, needs. You are alone, and you need to stop living for the pleasure of other people. At a minimum, this will give more respect to yourself. The more we say "No, I won't do it!", "I love like that, and I don't want to do anything else", "Let's do it my way this time," the more respect we get from those around us. Why? This suggests that "I value myself, respect and love, respectively, I want to be treated in this way." In fact, through our behavior we teach other people how to relate to us.

2. Defend your borders. If you do not want to do something for someone, you should talk about it.

3. It is important to focus on the ability to take attention, care, love, support and praise from other people. Only after you master and hone this skill, you can love yourself. Each person is a social being and grows his ego on the basis of other people's ego.

For example, I have a mother who respects and loves herself, men stare at her - that means, and I will behave this way in life. If my mother does not respect herself, feels like a victim, my behavior will be similar. However, in adulthood, you can choose another person whose ego can be relied on.

In the context of psychology, the psychotherapist, having special skills and knowledge, mirrors the person, so he can then accept and understand himself as he is, love and be proud of himself. The moment you have such a skill, you will not need to please other people to feel good - regardless of your behavior and decision (to please or not), your self-esteem will not change and your sense of confidence will only grow stronger inside your mind. If a stranger close to you is not close enough to you, you will not be able to believe him, because the ability to "take" and a sense of trust are disabled at a children's level. Where to look for the roots of this state? At the age of 3-5 years, the baby begins to perceive the maternal object in a different way. It implies any person from the environment of the child who raised and raised him was a very significant object, but at the same time appreciated and noticed only when the child was comfortable and did everything that was expected of him. For example, the baby was asked to behave quietly, play toys and not interfere, listen to mom's problems - and he meekly performed all this, trying to satisfy his attachment object, on which much depended on in his childhood. However, do not forget about the fact that now you are an adult and self-sufficient person, do not depend on anyone emotionally and materially - you rely only on yourself.

Naturally, in the life of every person there are socially significant personalities, but no one is ready to sacrifice their Ego and lose themselves, this is much more important than all that is happening around. It's not worthwhile to cultivate self-centered norms of behavior in yourself, it's nice enough to refuse a person, gently explaining: "This is more important for me now. Sorry, I do not reject you, I do not want to hurt you. First of all, I want to protect myself, to make something nice for myself. I'm tired and want to rest. " Failure does not mean that the world will reject you - others, on the contrary, will respect you as a person with their own opinions and views.

How to increase self-esteem after the betrayal of a husband / wife?

Treason is an event in a person's life that is always experienced quite difficult. First of all, it directly affects self-esteem. How to increase and strengthen it after such a tremendous shock in life?

1. Stop blaming yourself for what happened, for treason and betrayal. In this case, you are a victim. In general, there can be two main reasons for such a partner's behavior - his actions are partially justified by your behavior, and the partner is prone to cheating by nature. If a person is not happy with something in partnerships, he can directly say so or try to "reach out" to the consciousness of his partner in some other way. You are not directly guilty of such behavior, and self-flagellation will only complicate your situation and will further shatter the already unstable emotional balance.

You can carefully analyze the situation, recall certain moments of life together when you could not fully satisfy the needs and desires of a partner. However, for yourself it is worthwhile to understand that any person is not perfect and has every right to be incompetent in any issue / business. Perhaps you cannot give a person an all-consuming feeling of love or excessive care (these skills are not developed at a high level), and the partner is offended by not understanding the tone or reaction. Each person is individual, and it is important to choose a partner in life in accordance with his character and being. The ideal option is when people "get into the grooves" of each other's gears, but this does not always work. So, a partner may be dissatisfied with something, but you can express your dissatisfaction in various ways, and this is his direct fault, so be sure to let yourself get angry, throw out your resentment, express bitterness and resentment to friends and acquaintances - this is a completely normal reaction.

Guilt, on the contrary, destroys you from within, turning all the mobilized energy against yourself, causing yourself what you would like to do to the wrong partner (such a process in psychology is called retroflexion).

2. Do not compare yourself with a rival / rival. Perhaps in some ways she / he was better, but each of us has our own advantages and disadvantages. Treason is not due to the fact that someone's virtues are worse, but more disadvantages - these are completely unrelated things. You need to accept yourself, your strengths and weaknesses for granted. Confront with your negative thoughts.

For example: "This all happened due to a lack of attention on my part" - "I paid as much attention as I could; "It was necessary to hug and kiss him more" - "No, my affection and care was quite enough." You must clearly understand that at that moment you did everything possible, and this is not a reason for betrayal.

Responsibility for treason lies directly with the partner who has abused your trust. However, it should be clearly understood that to have confidence in someone does not mean to be weak and defenseless, therefore, you should not put an end to the sincerity and devotion of the opposite sex ("That's it. I won't trust anyone else!").

The one who betrayed is to blame, and there is nothing wrong with trusting your partner. The recognition of one's mistake before oneself is of no small importance ("Yes, I trusted this person!"), But then it's worthwhile to draw conclusions and learn to look at people before opening your soul.

3. Make a list of your strengths. Focus only on the good and the good that you have as an individual - what you do for other people, what you bring to the world, why you are such a wonderful person.

It is advisable to exaggerate all of its positive qualities, and it is better to make a new list every day (even if the points are repeated). The more recognition you give yourself, the less self-flagellation you will have.

4. Surround yourself with positive and optimistic people who can always protect you from negative thoughts, emotions and feelings, self-flagellation, will be glad to listen and help. In no case should you become locked in yourself - this is the period when a person needs contact most of all.

Find a patient friend who can listen to the same nagging for hours and repeat in response that your fault is not, you are worthy of love and trust. Often in such a state, a person does not have the strength to resist his own negative thoughts and words, so it's so important to have someone close to you who can support. Some people try to get away from thinking and worrying, surrounding themselves with a crowd that will entertain them. However, this is not a way out of the current situation - in this case it will be a crowding out of experiences, and they can drag on for years. We need to work on our impressions here and now - to analyze, relive, and draw the appropriate conclusions. The best option is to share experiences in contact with other people, then in your soul there will be less. Be sure to chat with the opposite sex (go on a date, flirt with someone, etc.).

If the relationship was broken, take some time to understand yourself and understand - who you like, what type you like, what qualities are your strengths and weaknesses. This approach will strengthen self-esteem, and the opinion of another person will not be reflected in it in any way.

You do not need to make the center of the Universe from your partner, concentrating all your supports and resources in it. The center of the universe must be in you! You should not be afraid of parting, especially if the partner hurts you - a worthy person can be found at any age, with any appearance and with any character.

It all starts with yourself - take for granted your strengths and weaknesses, characteristics in character and learn to respect yourself, do not take the blame on yourself and constantly develop self-esteem. It's difficult for some people to get to know themselves (if there is no mirroring), in which case they need a person nearby who will tell you what positive character traits they have ("But you are kind, warm, interesting, etc."), which is why many turn to psychologist - one session can turn your whole life upside down and make it an order of magnitude better!

5. Develop and learn something new. This is a wonderful period to learn something new, find yourself and understand what makes you get more energy.

Relatively speaking, development is that for which treason has occurred. As a rule, the experience of vivid emotions can become a kind of "awakening factor" in your life, you will begin to perceive yourself more realistically, decide on a hierarchy of values, understand what exactly you need from life, what is acceptable and bad, what life experience is worth repeating. Treason will allow you to analyze in detail the past and present of your soul, to rethink the values and moral approaches to life.

As a result, a person will never again allow to devalue himself as a person and trample his self-esteem. Yes, the experiences are painful, but you will not feel completely annihilated and amazed, and the awareness of your own "I" is preserved, thanks to a clear understanding of who I am, where I am coming from and in which direction I am moving.

In this way, identity is nurtured, because self-esteem is either increased or lowered, and the partner is just an indicator of it (if his actions are reflected in your self-esteem, then the problem arose much earlier).

How to love yourself?

Why don't you love yourself?

Questions of self-love are directly related to a person's self-esteem. How to learn to love yourself anew?

First you need to find a reason inside the subconscious that influenced the weakening of sympathy for your inner "I" - at some point in life you started to put pressure on yourself, and it is very important to understand when exactly this happened.
As a rule, people remember first the teenage years, then high school and junior school, and only then kindergarten and situations related to home education (this is the most difficult to remember).

If at school from classmates there was bullying, ridicule, boycotts, collective rejection, all this will necessarily affect the person's self-esteem and, accordingly, his love for himself. In addition, parents could exacerbate the situation by "adding fuel to the fire" (for example, comparing the behavior or achievements of their child with other children: "Look, John has good grades in mathematics! What are you? Look, Jane graduated from karate school with black belt! And you sit at home, do nothing! ". Such comparisons are put off in the psyche of the child, forming the feeling that they do not like and do not accept him.

Why do parents do this?

Mostly because of illiteracy in the field of child psychology.

Some are equal others try to show their children that they don't accept them, acting "on the contrary" (in reality, each parent wants his child to be better, but not everyone understands how to motivate the little one personality).

As a result, the child perceives a similar behavior in relation to himself as a manifestation of rejection and dislike on the part of the closest people, this feeling is realized but also firmly entrenched in his psyche. From this moment, he believes that love should only be earned, then you will deservedly be loved.

However, the family was given to us so that we would be loved, accepted and valued just like that, with all the shortcomings, flaws and irrepressible character. How else can dislike of oneself be connected with parents? Mom and Dad did not love and do not like themselves, respectively, because of the rejection of themselves, they do not accept a child. Relatively speaking, low self-esteem is passed down from generation to generation. For example, if a mother saw a deuce in her child's diary, she was primarily dissatisfied with herself, associating her dissatisfaction with her grandmother's behavior and expressing it to the baby.

What can still greatly affect a person's self-esteem and self-love? First love and failed relationship. As a rule, a feeling of first love occurs between the ages of 20-22. If a person is abandoned, he begins to blame himself - he did something wrong, problems with appearance (color of eyes, hair, etc.), the partner did not get what he wanted in the relationship. At this age, people are rarely able to soberly assess a multifactorial situation and understand that in reality it can be connected with the psyche. That is why they take the blame on themselves, causing another psychological trauma and lowering self-esteem. How to deal with the situation in general? Forgive all people who could put pressure on the wound (parents, classmates, first love). To do this, you need to remember all the painful situations and each offender (someone tore your backpack, someone threw a pencil case out the window, someone scoffed and looked contemptuously, and someone ridiculed your clothes and appearance). The trauma is deep enough, so it will be painful and scary to remember, right down to tears from a feeling of injustice (if that is so, this is a positive moment in therapy - the psyche unloads the trauma).

In addition, previously experienced emotions must necessarily appear - resentment, anger, disappointment. Find the right words (or actions) with which you could protect yourself at that moment. At this stage, you need to use your imagination and imagination - imagine that you really acted as the subconscious tells you now. From such actions, the psyche will receive great satisfaction, not as strong as with real actions, but 2-3 repetitions in the imagination may well calm the offense. See the desired reaction (that is, the face of your abuser).

All that you want to see, you need to try to imagine as bright as possible. It is important to understand that all the bad actions of people are associated with their heartache. As a rule, those who mock others at school experience bullying from their parents at home (both physically and mentally). This pattern of behavior is called acting out.

The child's psyche cannot endure stress for a long time (having experienced psychological or physical stress at home, he comes to school and spills his aggression on others in order to relax). Possessing all the psychological knowledge, it is enough to put pressure on your abuser to the sore spot to see his tears, disappointment, sadness and resentment ("Do you know what? You feel like a failure, you are bullied at home, so you do that!").

Get moral satisfaction, enjoy the moment of his triumph over the offender ("Great, and Julia became ill!").

Some people follow their offenders on social networks and rejoice at their failures and problems. This may satisfy for some time, so it is important to visualize the situation and unload it. If you experience a very deep resentment (but not at the stage of extreme bitterness), the following practice can sometimes help. Imagine that the offender apologized to you (What expression did he do? What did he say? How did he explain his behavior?).

This technique is perfect for parents, classmates, first love. However, in general, this is a very difficult and energy-consuming job, because psychologically we are afraid to look into the depths of our trauma, we experience an unconscious fear that we will not be able to cope with the surging pain, therefore, we need an accompanying psychologist or psychotherapist.

How else to learn to love yourself? First of all, watch your body, take care of it and give all the best that you can (as a mother takes care of her baby).

Quite predictable actions: - eat right; - Eliminate bad habits (tobacco and alcohol kill your body), but do not do it to the detriment of your psyche, sensations, emotional state and mood (if it's really difficult for you to refuse some food, let your psyche remain in a calm state); - do not sit on strict diets (one apple for breakfast, lunch and dinner), think about a balanced and harmonious diet; it is better to refuse several products (for example, one per month); - go in for sports, it's enough to even walk along the street an hour a day; - Each time, doing something for your body, say to yourself: "Look, this I do for you!".

Thus, you radiate goodness to yourself, and your body accepts this as love. - accept your body as it is (every fold, wrinkle, defect of the figure, etc.). Perhaps it is really ugly, there are problems with completeness, but it's all yours, and you live with it.

As a rule, we seize up some kind of stress and lack of positive emotions with food. - learn to forgive yourself, rethink all the mistakes you made in your life ("Well, at that moment I could only do that with my knowledge and experience. Now, when repeating the situation, I would have done everything completely different!");

-take yourself with all your shortcomings, do not compare yourself with other people (someone has a prettier face, but there are problems with deep mental trauma; someone writes beautiful texts, but does not know how to do anything with his hands - each of us has strengths and weaknesses); - constantly learn something new (a person who has mastered knowledge in a new field begins to love himself more and be proud of himself); -

learn to be proud of yourself and it doesn't matter that there are still many steps ahead to achieve the goal, because every small step, even the most insignificant, is already a victory worthy of pride. Definitely, any person in a year, five or ten years has any achievements.

Even if it seems to you that you have not done anything in life, look at your life through the eyes of another person.

For example, a businessman girl can envy a friend who has a spouse who provides her. And vice versa. -

 take it for granted and love your differences from other people ("Yes, I am such a person, I have such weaknesses, but I live perfectly with them!");

- drive away self-criticism and do not believe all thoughts that were formed earlier in your head (especially if you were often criticized by others around you as a child - otherwise, such thinking will develop in your head like weeds;

- figure out what exactly you really want (What do you want to try out of food? What do you want to wear? What words do you say to friends and relatives? What kind of people do you want to communicate with, and which ones to exclude from your circle of contacts?); -

stop talking with people who humiliate, insult and insult you, they treat you scornfully and indifferently - they simply suck your energy out. those who love and accept you can be supported and provided with a resource for further

advancement - do not let go of your passion and follow what you really like to do; find a business that will be fun (reading, drawing, talking with other people - if you get moral satisfaction, then at this moment you love yourself most);

- Everyday look for what you can be thankful for; - in times of crisis, in painful situations or in a bad mood, be sure to talk with family and friends, who are an additional psychological resource for you and support; - periodically disconnect from the outside world and go into yourself to search for your own resource;

- find a place where you will feel comfortable (home, cafe, restaurant, park, etc.), you can be filled with energy and go into yourself; - do not forget to have fun.

And most importantly, remember that you do not have to be an ideal superman, you can be an ordinary person with your own shortcomings and strengths. What you consider a disadvantage, someone else perceives as a huge resource!

How not to depend on the opinions of others?

What to do in situations where people close to you offer a joint rest, ask for something to buy, do for them or interfere in your life, trying to prove that you need to do what they think?

Often we simply can't answer in the answer: "No, I want it differently" or don't know how exactly we want it differently. However, fulfilling the desires of others, we certainly do not feel happy. To make the optimal decision, it is worthwhile to separate the issues of the material and psychological plan.

An example in the first case is buying a dress with a close friend, boyfriend or mother. Doubting your choice, you may ask: "Do you like more - a green or yellow dress?" However, having received the answer: "Green! It suits you that way, you look amazing! ", You don't feel the joy of the choice, but inside your consciousness tells you:" I don't even know ... No, not really! ". However, often in such situations, we agree with a loved one and ... buy a green dress. And then, going out into the street, we don't feel happy, there is no sensation of inner comfort, feedback from others and enthusiastic looks. Why? At a minimum, you do not like this green dress, you are unhappy with your choice, there is no delight from a perfect purchase. And it doesn't matter that in reality the green color suits you more! If in yellow you feel more comfortable, happier and happier, you should make a choice in his favor, because it is better to regret your choice, and not imposed by someone. Barren regret and a burning rebuke to oneself are always easier experienced than discontent and bitterness from the awareness of "manipulating" oneself as a loved one (in such a situation, these feelings will eat a person for a long time from the inside). When you choose just the wrong dress, you can throw it away and buy another one. We tried it, liked it, felt a sense of satisfaction ("Yes, yes! I want just that and like that!").

Seek, try your hand, test the possibilities, and sooner or later you will find what you want. If you keep following the wishes of other people all the time, you will never find yourself. Of course, there are different situations and friends, husbands / wives, mothers / fathers ("After all, I told you (a)!"), In this case we experience an acute sense of guilt. Now consider the psychological choice (relatively speaking - where to go for a walk, what profession or course to choose, where to study, how and with whom to celebrate a birthday, whether to help a girlfriend / friend if you need to do your business urgently). In fact, many people will postpone their studies and run to help, realizing that they will then feel bad because of this choice. Why is this happening and what is the basis of such dynamics of behavior?

As a rule, on a feeling of guilt (a person cannot understand where the boundaries of his responsibility and the responsibility of another person are). The psychological connection is as follows - if I refuse or choose something of my own, the person close to me will be upset, so I will feel guilty, due and I will have to quickly correct the situation to make it easier!

But it's worth understanding that what the other person feels is his personal responsibility, because in this way he gets his lesson in the process of communication with you. Alas, many people are accustomed to such a stable model of behavior. What to do in this case?

Remind yourself - "This is his responsibility!" Your direct responsibility is to properly explain to the person what is happening to him, why he was refused. For example, the answer to the phrase "I don't want to spend my free time with you today, I don't want to communicate either" can sound completely different:

- You know, today was a very difficult day for me. 8 clients, and everyone needed to get involved in the problem emotionally, plunging deep into their experiences and dividing them, so now I am exhausted energetically, my strength is at zero.

- I would really like to spend time with you, but not today - I feel bad.

- I would like to take a walk with you, but let's not go to the movies - I can't watch any films now.

- Let's go to the disco next time, and today we will spend time in a relaxed atmosphere.

Thus, a person needs to be made clear that no one is turning away from him: "I am not giving up on you. Today I choose myself, and these are completely different things. My behavior is connected exclusively with my psychological state at the moment. In our relations, nothing has changed, I still appreciate your opinion, respect you as a person and love. Moreover, I want to spend my free time with you. "

If a loved one cares about you, offering any global changes in life (for example, a change of profession, etc.), you can directly say: "Thank you for offering me various options, but there is no response in my soul. I am sure this is not my way. It is possible that you are right, and in a year I will regret my actions, but let me go this way on my own. It is very important for me!". You should not take responsibility for the pain of another person, but you must definitely keep in touch ("I'm really embarrassed to refuse you. It doesn't work again, and I understand that it's rather unpleasant for you, but now I can't"), recognizing the shackling guilt and shame. Relatively speaking, in an additional text we make it clear to a person that he is valuable and not indifferent, and the relationship is still preserved. As a result - he will not be so hurt and offended by the refusal, he will not be so frustrated.

A great example is a child who injured his knee. If the baby hit with his knee, and the mother did not react to his pain, did not show what she was experiencing, the situation would be more difficult to experience, and the pain would remain for several more years. If the child feels and sees that mother does not care, and it does not matter at all that she can do nothing, it's much easier to survive the painful sensations.

In the dynamics of people following their loved ones, a tendency is often traced - what is important to me and I want is not really valuable. Our relations with this person, his opinion, feelings and desires are much more valuable. People with similar problems can justify their actions with the following standard phrases: "When we are superficially familiar, I can quite talk about my feelings and do how comfortable for me.

If I am in a close relationship with someone, I try to be as convenient for this person as possible, so I want to create a comfortable relationship. " What could be the reasons for this line of behavior? The origins must be sought again in childhood - parents and others made the child comfortable for themselves, blamed for personal aspirations and desires bypassing their own interests, absolutely did not provide the opportunity to choose something of their own, violated his personal boundaries (could enter the room without knocking, demand that the baby does not close the door, otherwise they would cause a scandal).

As a result, already in adulthood, a person cannot understand what exactly he wants and, consequently, does not allow himself to establish these boundaries (simply close the door and say: "That's it! Do not enter here! This is my personal space, and here I want to be alone ! ").

How to deal with your own powerlessness?

First you need to regain the value of your desires, otherwise, going further on the occasion of all loved ones, a person begins to perceive such behavior in relation to himself as a manifestation of aggression (he has no responsibility for everything that he makes me do, there is only guilt, which means he is guilty!). Agreeing to fulfill the request of a loved one each time, a person begins to take offense over time, because he cannot take out aggression directly in contact, as a result, anger transforms into an insult and goes to himself ("That's it! They offended me! Nobody loves me. And he doesn't perceive me the way I want it!").

This stress factor begins to accumulate in the mind, holding on for some time in the psyche, and then acting out begins:

- You're tired of me, so don't call again! I do not want to talk to you!

- There may be a passive manifestation of discontent - "Well, we have come where you wanted!" Now bear my sour expression! " (in this case, you can feel the anger and irritation not hanging out in the air).

- A person may not answer the phone or "forget" to call, congratulate him on his birthday, fulfill his promise (there is so much aggression that this hostility fills 99% of the brain and supplants all good things).

So, what is the way out of this situation? The very first and most important thing is to understand what you want, the second is to give value to your inner aspirations, to realize that you yourself agree with such actions in relation to yourself and begin to voice personal desires to your loved ones. This is really important for a relationship, because in the end, by doing everything that a person does not want, and without objection, reconciling with everything, he will simply destroy the built relationship. To break this circle, first try a very simple exercise - say out loud "I would like to ...!". It doesn't matter if the phrase sounds quietly and not everyone hears it, the main thing is that you could say it out loud! You can say, "I dreamed. I saw it differently. "

If others are used to what you do as they feel comfortable, for the first time no one will hear you, but you should not stop - the water wears away the stone, so you need to talk, then offer, insist, demand, but do not stop. At a minimum, people will realize that not everything suits you. In addition, this approach will help not to break sharply the relationship.

In some situations, you will have to directly demand if others do not hear or do not want to hear. People are accustomed to such behavior, and you have such an attitude, choosing your environment so that it resembles childhood as much as possible, when you had to follow someone's orders and instructions.

Initially, when you chose an authoritarian person (perhaps a tyrant or a sadist) in your relations, you were very comfortable - he led behind him, managing everyone as puppets (including you). It is quite difficult to re-educate such a person, but it is worth the effort to satisfy your needs and close this level of mental development. In a comfortable relationship (when people have known each other for several years), it is also important to receive feedback from others, so you should not hesitate to ask about it, and if necessary, demand ("What do you think about this? Give me feedback! I need it ").

Over time, you will begin to be surrounded by individuals who know how to listen. Appreciate your needs and satisfy them, sometimes at the cost of relationships - we are all adults, and if a loved one is not able to help you satisfy your desires, why do you need relationships for the sake of relationships?

How to deal with perfectionism?

In psychology, perfectionism is the belief that the ideal can and must be achieved. How can perfectionism manifest itself?

 The fact is that a person, performing certain actions, will always observe himself from the outside and evaluate his behavior and himself as a whole (for example: "Did I write this word well? And this? And how does the whole phrase sound in a bunch? And the sentence in the text ?). As a result, in order to write one paragraph, a person can only evaluate himself from the outside for half an hour ("Is this good? And is this? And if I build the sentence this way?").

As a result, a huge amount of energy and energy is spent not only on the work itself, but also on the assessment of absolutely every word in the text, which is quite difficult to do.

What is a light technique? It is necessary to "turn on" the perfectionism mode later - to conduct an assessment after performing a certain piece of work.

At first you work as you can and how it turns out, and after a while (depending on the frequency of actions), for example, once a week or two weeks, conduct a "knowledge cut" to find bottlenecks that need additional editing and study. Then you should turn to someone who can help to deal with this skill, or work on the problem yourself by studying additional articles or watching a video.

However, it must be remembered that perfectionism is always accompanied by self-flagellation and self-abasement - "I am bad because I did so!". This line of behavior is fundamentally wrong - on the contrary, you need to develop more calm emotions for your actions, you must have a tolerant and respectful attitude towards yourself, you need to give yourself the right to make mistakes (this is normal, because a person is studying!).

And most importantly - you always need to remember that you want to become an order of magnitude better, but over time it will be!

How to stop envy?

Envy is a feeling that is customary to condemn, to be ashamed of, and not even admit to oneself in it. However, in reality, there are no bad feelings - they all signal to us something important.

What is the actual psychology of envy?

How to cope with this feeling?

Envy is conditionally divided into "white" and "black". What is the difference?

In the first case, this feeling absolutely does not harm others and constantly forces you to work on yourself, is aimed at internal self-improvement, and not at revenge on someone - "I envy this person and want to reach his level!". Examples of such envy: - in women: "Oh! What a beautiful long hair she has! I'll also grow myself like that! " - in men: "Oh! My friend bought a new car! I'll definitely buy the same one! " Accordingly, a person gradually begins to move towards achieving a goal, for example, to earn more (he knows that in a year or two he can afford the same car as his friend).

Difficulties begin when envy turns black. When does this happen?

At that moment when there is a desire to destroy the object of envy or to make it as bad as the envious person himself. In this state, a person completely relieves responsibility for everything that happens in his life, believing that it is the object of envy that is the cause of his own failures and humiliation.

In other words, this condition can be characterized by one exact phrase - "We do not need anything, if only others had nothing!". For example, I want to reach the level of Bill Gates, but with my income below the average, I need to work a hundred years and it is unlikely to reach this level - the gap is too big! In this case, a feeling of envy begins to torment a person, destroy and "eat" him from the inside. What to do in this situation?

First you need to study the person to whom envy arose, to find out some negative aspects of his life - as a rule, there is a certain price that people pay for their lives. For example, stars cannot go outside without makeup (especially girls), cannot retire somewhere in the city - a journalist can watch over, take a picture, and the next day a completely unsightly photo will appear in the newspapers. There are drawbacks in wealth - a person must constantly think about the security of his money (Where to invest? Which bank is more stable for storage?).

Another example, more mundane and vital. One friend is jealous of the second that she has been married for many years, her husband provides her with everything, and in general she has a strong and friendly family. However, in reality there may be a reverse situation - marriage is not so good (a woman is forced to endure her husband, who is always dissatisfied with everything).

We can envy the ideal image, but looking deeper, everything may turn out to be completely different from what it seems at first glance - a person can have serious problems. To analyze what exactly one likes in a person attracts appearance, money, fame or property (a beautiful car, apartment or house). Then we think deeper. Do you like the way he makes money? What skills do you have? Or the ease with which he succeeds in everything in life? All these points are very important to indicate - what exactly and how you like it. You can't just dwell on one picture - "He has a good car, I want one too!"

If a person does something that is so hooked on in another (for example, he buys a car), it won't become any easier — he engages and catches something deeper. As a rule, with a thorough analysis, you can find something really important and valuable for you. Of course, not everyone can become the second Bill Gates, but everyone can give himself the right to achieve at least something. The main thing is to understand the essence of your envy. In this case, the process of reflection will be "curative", the worldview will change, a person will not be so "thrown" with envy: "He's so cool, but I'm nothing!" However, living with such beliefs is quite difficult - if you do not return to reality and start moving, you can just freeze in one place. If you like something, do it! In life, everything is possible. When a person really wants something, he will certainly achieve it. Perhaps he does not gain all the glory of the world, but moving in the right direction can achieve great heights. The main thing is to go to that image, which is the object of envy, because this is just what you want. But do not choke on the path to your ideal - in reality, everything is always ambiguous (there is no only white or black, only good or bad).

Life is like a labyrinth - the whole path is twisted (something will be good, but something bad). That is why if envy is divorced from reality, it is very painful.

How to survive treason, betrayal, loss and start living?

If a person asks the question "How to live further?", Probably he had to endure a strong and traumatic psyche shock - the loss of a loved one (or parting), favorite work, business, which was associated with a lot of hopes, betrayal or any other events that "knocked out" from under the ground. " How to protect yourself in such situations and get out of a state of shock and psychological stress?

First of all, you need to abandon any rash and harsh actions and "lay low." Quite often, people under emotional influence begin to recoup on others, trying to hurt them, or make themselves suffer physically. In a state of severe shock, you can make many mistakes not only in your life. That is why you just need to allow yourself to live (eat, sleep, chat with loved ones, do not forget about personal hygiene), and the soul to relax during this time. Lack of proper self-care and proper sleep can lead to more serious health problems, including depression. When the pain begins to subside, the question arises - how to live on?

The process of overcoming the state of shock can be compared with the beginning of a new life, and at this stage it is important to believe in yourself and your abilities, start setting goals, dreaming about something.

You can imagine your future (for example, in six months - depending on what stage of the experience of the event the person is). If painful memories begin to fade, this is a signal to move on - to dream, plan, set goals and move towards their implementation. At this stage, it is important to perceive everything conceived as completely feasible and commensurate with its capabilities. A person must understand that changes in life will be, they are possible and will definitely happen. Periodically, memories will pop up, this is quite normal, even if pleasant or bad snippets of the experienced situation are in your head - remember, cry, be sad or wallow in bed from impotence. It is important to receive and give emotions, therefore it is necessary to find an interlocutor with whom you can discuss everything experienced, talk, cry.

Sometimes, on the contrary, you need a person to talk on abstract topics in order to "go out" into the real world or just keep quiet. The next step is to learn to enjoy and enjoy the little things (for example, delicious food - ice cream, fruit, meat). Eat and enjoy it - this is life. What else can cause positive emotions? Flowers, warm sunshine, beautiful pictures on the Internet, an interesting film, a walk in the park, pet. Over time, you need to try something new, look for yourself in creativity, attend classes that will give pleasure and enjoyment.

The most important thing is never to give up. You can worry, cry, be sad, but you can't give up - life is not finished and you need to move forward.

Having coped with such a life crisis, a person becomes stronger, and in the future it will be easier to survive the shock. What else can help? It is advisable to recall not only the event that caused the recent shock, but also previous crises in life when something like this happened. What resources helped manage stress? Who was nearby? How did you overcome previous crisis conditions - perhaps you did nothing and rested for several months, tried to distract yourself, or, conversely, filled all your free time with your favorite pastime? It is important to understand that if I survived the previous shock, then I can now.

Life is full of crises - small and large. They happen regularly, and people are often in crisis all their lives, not suspecting that they can live differently.

You should not be afraid of crises; they, like signal lights, indicate that the time has come for changes, without which a full-fledged life is impossible.

But what kind of changes is a question for each of us personally, and we must answer it ourselves without help and clue. The crisis says that it is time to stop, look back, carefully evaluate the present and revise the future. The crisis is an impetus for further growth. Surviving this condition is difficult, but quite real.

How to identify a liar?

How to determine that a person is cheating, and understand the reasons for cheating? The following signs of deception can be distinguished:

1. A person can confusely speak, stutter, repeat the same word or phrase several times.

2. A person does not look directly at the interlocutor, lowers his eyes to the floor or looks away. This is usually from shame.

3. Talk about nothing, a lot of extra phrases that distract from the main topic.

4. Quite often, liars use the phrase "Okay, I'll tell you", then tell some part of the truth or invent a temporary excuse (the "indirect" truth is not so terribly scary to tell) to hide the main essence of fraud.

5. A noticeable tension in the body (but this is not always a clear lie) - shoulders often rise, one can observe closed poses.

6. Quick answer to questions - a person has pre-thought out and prepared blanks for answer options. In general, there are no exact methods for defining deception - all people are different (some are sensitive to the incriminating tone (they are shy, afraid, ashamed), therefore they start to behave as if they are deceiving. Why does the desire to deceive arise? Often this is the person's protective mechanism - he he is afraid that he will be punished for his actions; blames himself for bad actions that can lead a partner or other people into a frustrating state (anger, sadness, resentment, etc.); ashamed of having ruined his ideal self-image. the issue of pair relations. The most important aspect is the partner's reaction to the truth (if it's not safe to tell the truth to one of the partners, he will cheat.) There is a category of people who are used to constant deception at every step - nothing will happen if the truth is slightly embellished. The root of the problem in this case, you need to look in early childhood - in the maternal object.If the child did something wrong as his parents wanted it, blamed him, they were ashamed or often punished, often beyond measure. As a result of this injustice, the child began to deceive his parents and, as an adult, continues to lie. Thus, a person protects himself. In general, to understand by external signs a person is cheating or not is difficult enough. But do we always need to know the truth?

If a person is not ready to hear the truth, it is better not to ask. There are people who need to find out the truth by any means in order to control the situation, so they are interested in all the little things (Did it exactly? And how did it, right? What did you say, why did you react like that?). For another person, this may sound like an attack, so he begins to defend himself and his dignity through deception.

In addition, there is another protective function of deception - one participant in the dialogue wants to protect the second from pain. Thus, it is possible to determine whether a person is deceiving by signs of guilt, shame and fear on his face. Perhaps in the depths of consciousness there is fear associated with individual experiences.

However, one must remember that all people are different, each has certain character traits and a line of behavior. The best option is to listen to your intuition in each case.

In addition, the following fact should be taken into account - if a person has convinced himself of what he is deceiving, those around him will never guess about the deception.

How to protect yourself from aggression?

How to protect yourself in a situation where unfamiliar people show aggression in a team new to you or even in line? What is the essence of the problem, and why has there been more aggression in your life?

As a rule, outbursts of aggression and hostility from others always indicate that inside the person himself there is a lot of aggression - we notice only what is inside of us from the outside.

There is a wonderful defense mechanism - projection. Almost all of life is built on the principles of projection (in the world of psychology, this is 100%). That is why, if it seems that people around are evil, and only ill-will show in their actions, it is worth asking yourself - where is the anger in me?

In some situations, anger can be a reaction to the frequent violation of personal boundaries. Relatively speaking, the psyche itself unconsciously requires intervention in the inner world of the personality, provokes others to invade. At the same time, a person can do absolutely nothing, and no emotions will even be reflected on his face. Where does aggression come from?

This may be a manifestation of children's hostility towards their guardians (mother, father, grandfather, grandmother, etc.); in response to any type of border violation, evidence that at the moment the person is very vulnerable and vulnerable. Perhaps a person has undertaken an in-depth study of his psyche, in which case weaknesses appear in the mind, and any approach is perceived by the person quite aggressively, so often you want to push the "offender" - "Go away and do not touch me!".

If strangers touch a sick person's consciousness, you should ask yourself: "Which of the close relatives (spouses, parents, children, brothers and sisters) resemble the" offender "in behavior or even in appearance, what kind of unconscious response does it cause?" For example, this may be due to the mother and her attempts to influence the actions of the individual. In such a situation, the root of aggression lies behind the maternal figure, so it's worthwhile to study this problem in detail (Why did you get angry? What was not said and what I would like to say?). A temporary solution to the problem is acting out on other people (I will express myself to this person, and my anger will pass). However, such behavior leads to rather negative consequences - there is a desire to recoup even more, over time it will look like psychopathy and narcissism.

It can be quite difficult to independently diagnose a high level of aggression, rage, anger and dissatisfaction. Why? If a person has lived his whole life with some degree of aggression and internal tension, he does not know and does not understand the difference. However, defending one's life from moral monsters is not an option, therefore, at least, one should ask about the origins of the emergence of internal aggression.

There are periods in life when some kind of emotional wound hurts more, in such cases you always unconsciously want to defend yourself and get moral, even sadistic, satisfaction from what has hurt another. And sometimes there are so-called healing periods (a kind of compensation for all years of suffering). At this time, a person can know himself better, understand the roots of his aggression and opportunities, be vulnerable next to someone and find inner balance. Alternatively, you can push everyone away from yourself, it hurts to do in response. However, this will not get better forever, this is a standard way to prove to your psyche that you can completely protect yourself, that there is a strong personality inside you that can refuse or, on the contrary, take whatever you want from life. Every day is competition in any case, and aggression is a way to satisfy one's needs, especially if a person hid all his life. How to understand that aggression was suppressed over a long period of time?

In this case, an inner stiffness is felt. If we are talking about some kind of action, a person is embarrassed, compressed, unconsciously trying to hide. In situations where there is aggression and aggressors, the psyche tries to convey that it is time to throw out everything that has accumulated outside.

How to protect yourself from aggressive attacks? You can enable retaliatory aggression and respond accordingly. However, it's not so much the behavior that matters more than the inner feeling that the individual makes a clear distinction between the aggressor and himself ("He will not take away my energy, I won't allow him!"). The most acceptable phrases are "No, I don't need this!", "Leave me alone, please," "I am not interested in this right now," "I would not want to discuss this topic with you." If a person can respond calmly and confidently to all provocations, this indicates that his internal level of aggression has fallen.

It is important that the answer confirms the inner desire of the individual - "No!" means no! (and not "Maybe," "Someday," "Maybe," "Try again, later.") If the aggressor makes repeated attempts, this completely contradicts the words of the person, respectively, in all non-verbal manifestations he hears "Yes!" Thus, this will indicate that within the consciousness of a person cannot refuse to satisfy someone's needs. To counter such manipulations, it is necessary not only to work out a line of behavior, but also to find the internal state.

At the first stage, it is necessary to clearly and confidently learn to say "No, I will not do it!", "Do you know what? This is my life, it's up to me to decide what I will do and what not! ","" I cannot allow you to do this! " Then you need to realize and find the internal state of aggression, feel how everything is bubbling and boiling inside - while outwardly it is necessary to maintain complete calmness, emotions should not be reflected on the face.

It is also important to understand the system of personal boundaries - what can a person allow others to do in relation to themselves? To do this, you need to analyze all painful life situations and make a list. Anger is always a contact feeling.

That is why, if it arises, this is a sign that the person was not satisfied in a certain contact or the connection was broken. First of all, to understand the root of the problem, it is necessary to analyze close relationships and the childhood period - as an option, not enough warmth and support was received.

How to return sex to a long relationship?

Indeed, over time, sexual desire may fade, rarely occurs, sometimes sex may be completely absent.

This problem worries many couples, and in order to understand it, it is necessary to find out the possible reasons for the lack of sex in a relationship.

First of all, partners need to accept the fact that there is a problem and clarify for themselves what is happening in the relationship (sexual relations have become rare, absent or generally do not satisfy one of the partners).

In its psychology, sex resembles the psychosomatics of the couple's body, respectively, is a symptom of a relationship disorder. Quite often, the basis of rare sexual relationships or their absence may be accumulated resentment, anger, dissatisfaction.

For example, a woman likes pleasant signs of attention on the part of her partner (romantic dates, courtship, flowers, gifts (even insignificant)), but the man ceases to take such steps, as a result - her sexual desire decreases, and dissatisfaction builds up. The opposite situation - the partner may be offended by the fact that he is given very little time (a woman works a lot, trying to fulfill herself in the professional sphere, devotes all her free time to her hobby and is not at all interested in the emotional side of personal relationships).

The result will be similar - a man loses sexual attraction to a woman. There can be many options for mutual insults in a pair.

The second fairly common reason for the lack of sex in a couple is a strong merger of partners (partners are always together, do everything together, have the same hobbies). In this case, over time, one of the partners gets tired of this, gets fed up, begins to feel that he does not have free space. As a result, sex (like the peak of a merger) becomes uninteresting and can even cause disgust. The third reason is that one of the partners has a feeling of shame much stronger than sexual desire (he is ashamed, embarrassed, afraid to liberate himself in order to get full satisfaction from sexual relations).

Accordingly, this also affects his interest in this area - a person closes in his problem and refuses sex. In any of the three cases, it is necessary to initiate a conversation on the topic of intimate relations, during which you need to gently find out the true reasons for the lack of sexual desire in the partner.

It is necessary to talk about grievances, irritation, anger, dissatisfaction, and difficulties in emancipation. In general, talking alone can help. It is also very important to understand which particular area of dissatisfaction affects relationships. How to renew interest in the intimate sphere of partners? What techniques and exercises can I use?

1. "Yin and Yang" - one of the partners takes a dominant position in the relationship, the second submits, then vice versa.

2. In the case of severe violations in the intimate sphere, many sexologists suggest a couple for several months to exclude the usual sexual intercourse and caresses of the genitals. In this case, partners can caress each other in other parts of the body. A similar approach is used to restore the sensual part in the relationship of the couple, to find other erogenous points. In long-term relationships, there are frequent cases when partners are exclusively interested in the instinctive satisfaction of their needs, forgetting about the emotional component and that satisfaction can be obtained from ordinary touches.

3. Sex without sound (for example, partners are afraid that they will be heard by passers-by, neighbors, parents).

4. Sex with eyes closed.

5. Porn roulette - open at random any porn video and try to repeat their actions after the actors. This is not always real, but in general, many couples perceive such a game is quite interesting.

6. Role-playing games with dressing up in costumes.

7. Sex without kisses (if it is customary for a couple to kiss a lot, you can exclude for a while (or reduce) this component of intimate relationships) can give a sense of sensation.

8. Directly during intercourse, you can practice telling your partner various vulgar words. If you make an effort, an intimate life can be restored, but it all depends on both partners. If in a couple someone is not ready to try to understand the essence of the problem, to listen and try something new, this indicates a great dissatisfaction in the relationship.

How to overcome the fear of rejection?

Every person at least once in his life experienced a fear of rejection, rejection and self-expression. For example, fear of receiving a refusal when meeting someone, in a proposal to meet and spend an evening together (that is, any refusal that is possible in a relationship between a man and a woman).

This category also includes the fear of being rejected as a person, that is, the fear of self-expression (counter-negativity, criticism and aggression in response to any actions of a person and his desire to prove himself), and fear of asking for help from a loved one or partner. So how is the fear of rejection formed?

This condition is formed in early childhood. A small child is already a person with his needs for emotional contact. However, close people (in most cases, maternal and paternal figures), as well as other relatives who raised a child (grandparents, aunts, uncles) and mentally replaced their mother, could be cold with him, that is, they emotionally and physically rejected the baby. They did not perceive him as an individual, an

Individual with their needs and desires, did not reckon with his borders. What is this line of behavior expressed in? When the baby approached people important to him (emotionally) for warmth and tenderness, to be stroked and soothed, paid attention, listened, he was refused. The most common answers in this case are "Leave me alone!", "Don't you see? I'm busy now! "," Oh my god, what a stick you are! "

This also includes the rejection of children's desires (for example, a child wants to watch one cartoon, but they put him completely different, etc.). Thus, personal needs were not taken into account, the attitude was cold, dismissive and indifferent.

Perhaps now a person does not remember who and how exactly belonged to him, since such experiences belong to an early age (from 2 to 5 years), many of them could be replaced by the psyche, as they were unpleasant. However, the soul remembers and, if you ask this question, you can answer it yourself. Why?

The thing is that the behavior of the educating person has not changed - he does not see the personality in his pupil, tries to advise something all the time (regardless of whether the advice is suitable), constantly repeats: "So I said (a), and again you are doing wrong! " Since the man was rejected several times in early childhood, he suffered a mental wound in this place, so he simply stopped all attempts to satisfy his emotional needs. Moreover, many began to consider their emotional desires as something bad, wrong, indecent, shameful.

However, all the memories based on the experienced emotions remained at heart. That is why, having matured, a person is psychologically imprisoned for rejection, sometimes even in those cases when he is not. Friends, partners - from all he feels a certain rejection, neglect of his personality. Sometimes people with a similar mental problem see rejection in each partner's action or unconsciously choose rejecting and cold partners who will not value them as a person. Why?

The thing is that they have a strong and uncontrolled internal drive to reject, something seems to catch fire in their souls, and they become dependent on the person who rejects them. In an attempt to get love, attention and care from a partner, which at one time the parents did not give, the rejected and mentally suffering person will tolerate further rejection, actually begging for a different attitude.

In this case, it's a "funnel of injury" - a person experiences experiences like children's, they reject him, this is unpleasant and embarrassing, but feelings remain. That is why he must do everything that he could not do in childhood with mom and dad - he must make his partner show love, care and attention. Such an incomplete gestalt can be repeated many times - this will not work, then there will be the next, the next ...

Quite often there are situations when a person with a trauma of rejection still gets attention and care, the partner becomes uninteresting to him, so he goes to another. The reason for this behavior is that incomplete gestalt in partnerships is rarely satisfied, since this is an underlying children's need. How to fix this fear of failure? How to deal with it? First of all, you need to realize the trauma of rejection, to recognize it.

It is useful to understand from whom exactly and how the rejection was received, so you can figure out what kind of transfer is carried out on the partner (for example, looking at the partner, you can see the rejecting mother). Having carefully assessed the current situation and thought about who could cause the trauma of rejection, a person will surely understand everything according to his feelings, since despite the fact that the brain is trying to supplant this pain, the soul remembers it. Who was cold in childhood and cold now? Who does not perceive you as a person, constantly teaches you to live, constantly criticizes for any independent step?

At heart, a person knows the answer to this question - mother, father, grandmother or grandfather. Learn to understand the real rejection of others and the moments of getting into the "funnel of injury". How to do it? It is necessary to soberly assess the behavior of a person, perhaps he did not want to offend and injure anyone, just some of his words resemble the phrases of his mother, father, grandmother or grandfather.

Quite often this happens, so our consciousness interprets this as a rejection. To control your communication with rejecting people, to minimize it, so as not to inflict repeated trauma on yourself. You should not build further romantic and friendly relations with them. If a person fell into the "funnel of injury", the rejection of the partner or others was not real, you need to repeat to yourself again and again that the situation was subjective, in fact, rejection seemed. Find friends and enlist their support. In the immediate environment there should be 1-2 people who respect you as a person and appreciate, accept with all the flaws and positive qualities, never rejected.

The main task is to learn to rely on such people, if necessary, ask for help, trust them. They will help to understand the current situation and understand whether the rejection seemed or is it really real.

It is quite difficult to independently deal with the rejection injury (real or far-fetched). What could be the difficulty? First of all, it is difficult for an outcast person to believe that someone can perceive him as he is. In addition, traumatized individuals have a lot of anxiety, so it is quite difficult to cope alone. In the zone of rejection trauma, there is nothing more effective than psychotherapy, since the therapist will help to understand whether the current situation is real, reduce the anxiety state, and give a new experience of acceptance (seeing that someone accepts the person as he is, he will be able to accept yourself), will not allow you to again establish a relationship in which the client will receive repeated injury. Of course, the psychotherapist will not hold hands from any act, but the inner awareness that the rejection situation is repeating at the moment, an uncontrolled drive is turned on, will make the person move on.

Psychotherapy will also help dispel false and causeless anxiety, the emotional stress of injured individuals, which they almost always experience. Knowing the characteristics of the client's character, the therapist can choose the appropriate mantras that need to be repeated many times to anxious people.

Example of a mantra: "No, they did not reject me, it just seemed to me. No, they didn't reject me, it just seemed to me. Go check it out. Go check it out. Go ask. "

Such an appeal to oneself significantly affects the mind and emotions, helps to calm down. Due to the fact that the traumatic is emotionally unstable, and he has a lot of anxiety in terms of rejection, a self-fulfilling prophecy begins to work. What does this mean? A man with his unconscious actions does everything to be rejected. It is difficult to constantly be in a state of anxiety, for such people it is better to be rejected, in which case they will rest and stop thinking about whether they are rejecting or accepting them at the moment.

However, one must remember: the more traumatic injured in the rejection zone, the more people will reject it. The society is organized in this way - we unconsciously feel a person's fear and do what the person is most afraid of. In addition, the traumatic person himself provokes a similar attitude towards himself - leave me, reject me. However, deep down, he most of all wants to not be rejected and tolerated as he really is.

The problem is that a person simply does not know how to do this. In psychotherapy, the client receives a new experience when he is not rejected for any character traits and actions, specific relationships with people, accepting as he is. Quite often, the traumatic person checks his partner for stability, sometimes these checks are very stringent.

Therapy from real life differs only in that the psychotherapist, having special skills and understanding the depth of the problem, does everything in order not to injure the person. Regardless of the person's attempts to do everything so that the attitude towards him changes radically, he is rejected, the therapist will not change his attitude.

However, the moment of healing will come only when the traumatic person accepts himself for who he is. It is after gaining new experience in contact with another person and having understood his deep "I" that the client will be able to move on. There are situations when, after prolonged therapy, moments of a "funnel of injury" still occur. This is not entirely true - just a person experiences similar experiences. If you do not try to hide these feelings away in the soul, pushing them to the background, and analyze the current situation, you can "treat" this painful sensation. As a result, a person will understand what to do in such cases. As an example, consider the following situation. A person in the past has a trauma of rejection, he finds himself in a similar situation. In order to dispel your doubts and conjectures, you need to get feedback from those people who, in his opinion, can be rejected. How to do it? To ask interesting questions directly: "It seemed to me? What was it? Tell me how you feel about me? Tell me, my act was very scary? After that, will everyone hate me? " A direct conversation like this can be very helpful. What else can help?

At the moment, when a person faces his fear of rejection, he must remember that he is not facing his mother, father, grandfather or grandmother. Perhaps this person will turn out to be completely different, respond to the need for love, friendship and care, appreciate the warm attitude to himself. Accordingly, when the traumatic feels that he is being rejected, he needs to remind himself that there is not a maternal or paternal figure nearby, that these are just memories of children's experiences when he felt unnecessary and was ashamed of his actions. The person who is nearby is completely different.

In fact, emotional attachment, the need for love and care are natural. If you have been rejected today, it's just one person's refusal, and it doesn't mean the rejection of the whole world. Tomorrow this person will forget about his act, so you need to go further. A very important aspect in working out the fear of rejection is to believe in and fall in love with the idea that there are people in the world who are ready to respond to the warmth and want to give their care and support in return. When a person believes in this idea, fear will become less.

Fear of failure is also associated with a strong need for someone or something, so strong that it becomes a painful addiction. Do not invest all your love, care and support in one single person. After all, the desired warm feelings can be obtained from several people - friends, relatives, work colleagues, etc. It is absolutely not scary to lose people who do not correspond to the soul. It is scary when one person personifies the whole universe. However, you can not live with a person, playing a role. This is impossible - in the end, no one will be happy. In this world there are different people who want and can give love, care and support (and these are not necessarily relatives). You just crossed at some point and the person liked.

Another reason for the fear of failure is fear of shame. A sense of shame is necessary in order to socialize in the environment, to act in accordance with the norms and principles of society. When a person receives a refusal in response to his warmth, there is a feeling that he is doing something wrong. This feeling is so deep and all-consuming that quite logical conclusions arise:

"My actions are wrong. I am bad because I want love, care and attention. " But this is not so. Any person deserves a good attitude towards himself. It is just that one who is not injured in the rejection zone, believes that he will have love and attention, does not focus on rejecting individuals, but goes to those who are ready to give him what they want.

So, the most important life attitudes for a traumatic in a rejection zone:

Take yourself and your needs for love, care and attention for granted.

Stop self-flagellation - anyone deserves a warm attitude.

Find a person who is willing to share his warmth in return.

How to keep a relationship happy?

The biggest and most powerful landmine in the relationship is the illusion that there are no problems if they are not discussed by partners. One of the features of our upbringing is that conflicts must be avoided, all problems should be hushed up, less complaints and more smiles (in general, "avoid sharp corners").

The person who copes with this task perfectly is considered in our society a kind of "ideal", others want to communicate with him. And vice versa - those people who are constantly voicing their problems, are ready to understand the causes of the troubles and conflicts that have arisen, to correct something in their lives, are sometimes considered moral freaks, they are less loved, they do not take into account their opinions, and criticize life views. Often this attitude is found in married couples in which there are problems, and one of the partners is not silent, but is trying to speak out. Talking about problems, dissatisfaction in relationships, needs is much more effective than keeping silent.

The more partners are silent, the more the problem is aggravated (resentment (obvious and implicit) accumulates in the soul, anger and irritation to the partner increase), as a result, relationships worsen, people cease to understand the true causes of quarrels. The situation resembles a huge ball of thread, which is simply impossible to unravel together. Due to the understatement and suppression of their thoughts, the gap between the partners is only growing, they are gradually moving away from each other. As a result, such a moment may arise when mutual misunderstanding reaches its peak, strength and energy run out and prove something and try to fix it.

If a couple has encountered such a problem, it is worth contacting a therapist and take a course of family psychotherapy. The therapist in this case acts as a stable figure that stabilizes the situation. In addition, he will help unravel the tangle of mutual insults and feelings, relieve tension in relationships and teach you to understand each other at a deep level. This will eliminate the perception of an ordinary request or complaint of dissatisfaction with something in the relationship as a claim. A partner may feel guilty or shame because of a reproach towards him, therefore, he defends himself in response, not understanding the true cause of dissatisfaction.

There can be two options:

The partner resists because of his guilty feelings or the accumulated negative childhood experience - in this case, each reproach is perceived as a kind of shame. One of the partners may be dissatisfied by humiliating the human dignity of the second (derogatory statements, actions, etc.).

In this case, one must take into account the following nuance - if one destroys the dignity of his partner, he will no longer be able to trust, speak openly about his feelings, and may respond unconsciously with barbs in response to comments. Be sure to carefully pay attention to any statement of the partner, to his tone of voice. Men talk about their dissatisfaction, needs and emotional experiences often little and quietly. If you skip a disgruntled word one, two, three times, they simply cease to open their souls and share their feelings and opinions related to relationships.

Accordingly, discontent and irritation will accumulate, manifesting itself in the form of ridiculous aggressive actions towards each other. As an example, we can consider a fairly simple situation - the partner (spouse) does not wash a mug after morning coffee. Such an attitude can annoy the second partner, the irritation will accumulate and eventually spill over into a flash of anger. However, to prevent a conflict, it's enough to talk with a person and show your displeasure: "Honey, could you wash a mug?" If time passes, the situation repeats, the conversation can be repeated: "Why didn't you wash the mug? I asked you. " Why is it important to talk about everything? A frank conversation gives the partner an understanding that efforts are being made to take his actions, there are certain feelings and discontent.

In the end, you can understand the reason for the actions of a person - for example, in childhood in his family it was customary to wash dishes in the evening or in turn by someone from the family. If the current situation does not suit one of the partners, a compromise must be sought.

In any case, no matter what decision would be made, the person will be aware that his action (did not wash the cup) will cause internal stress, so he will try to change his behavior.

Thus, in communication, open communication is necessary, this is the first step to achieving harmony and mutual understanding.

Do not pretend that everything is in order, if something does not suit and annoy you, avoid complicated conversations - this is the way that will lead to a dead end.

How to find peace of mind?

 If a person asks about how to find peace of mind, it is logical to assume that at the moment he is restless in his soul.

There can be two reasons: There is a void on the soul that crushes and makes one suffer — there is nothing to "catch on" to.

The soul is a heavy burden.

In this case, you need to understand what specifically gnaws to dump this load and fill the void with something important.

There is an interesting and quite effective tactic developed by the Eastern monks. Its essence is to always be in the present, here and now. In most cases, our thoughts are in the past, in the future, or in fantasies. That is why such flights of our consciousness in the end can cause anxiety and many negative feelings. If a person is here and now, he cannot be bothered by anything. How to achieve this state?

Everything is simple - performing any action, you need to fully concentrate on it, immerse yourself in it.

For example, eating. It is necessary to develop your own ritual. If the esthetic side is important for a person, you need to choose the most beautiful dishes that he has. If you like to cook, then you should cook the dish yourself. But at the very moment of cooking, when performing simple actions (peeling vegetables, the cooking process, adding odorous spices), every second you need to think only about food.

The most important part of this ritual is eating directly. You need to fully concentrate on the process, to feel every moment - how the food enters the mouth and, in contact with the tongue and saliva, begins to dissolve. What is the taste of food - sweet, salty, bitter, spicy or spicy? All this can be felt, but every minute thoughts will still try to escape into the past and present - how was the day, what will happen tomorrow? You need to try to go back to the present and focus on eating and your inner sensations. A similar exercise can be performed every day. And it doesn't matter what it will be - a meal or some other conscious action. It is important to find for yourself 10-15 minutes a day to live in the present tense, here and now. When cleaning the apartment, you can only think about the cleaning process itself, about every item that is rearranged. Laying clothes in shelves in the closet, you can also consciously be here and now, feel the touch of the fabric, its texture. Walking in the park or returning home, you can ask yourself the question "What am I doing and what do I feel?". The more such moments there will be in a person's life, the calmer he will have in his soul.

The emotional burden will pass over time, unless a person consciously passes it through the prism of his perception - in this case, the feeling of heaviness will only intensify.

However, in fact, the cargo refers to the past or future, but it does not matter for the present.

How to find your meaning in life?

Questions about the meaning of life are raised in most cases in situations where people are not satisfied with something. If everything is in order and goes on, nobody asks similar questions. The question of the meaning of existence arises when a person is in a state of deep psychological discomfort or existential crisis, which may be accompanied by life crises - loss of work, divorce, birth or departure of children from the family. In such periods, the question arises of what to do next and how to live. Often a person wants to completely reconsider his life.

So how to find your own meaning of existence? All questions about the meaning of life ultimately come down to finding oneself, to feel one's worth and to enjoy life.

To solve these problems, you can set goals and achieve them, however, if they do not fall into the value range of a certain personality (Vasya and Petya succeeded, and I want to!), The crisis will worsen even more, a person will not get satisfaction from life, and will again ask questions about the meaning of existence. Why?

Because by and large, we all want to be happy, and the question of the meaning of existence can be reformulated - "How to become happy?" Thus, if you look at life so existentially, you need to understand that there is only one outcome for any person - a small "home" for the body, located somewhere 2 meters underground. That is why only the quality of life and emotions matters, for some people - the quality of communication, contact with others. In general, every minute of existence should be filled with emotional outbursts.

Psychologists recommend breaking down all the meanings of life into 3 main categories: - material; - emotional; - spiritual. The first category includes the ability to earn a certain amount of money in a chosen way. Money alone cannot be the meaning of life, otherwise a person would not think about such issues. In the material sense, for many the skill that is pumped during making money, the process itself, through which this material good is earned, is of great importance. Money and security are the foundation of our life, an important and integral component. Where to live and what to eat are the main tasks, without which it is simply impossible to think of something else.

Thus, the satisfaction of the simplest but most vital needs is the first step towards understanding the meaning of existence.

The emotional meaning of life is the whole depth and totality of human experiences. Emotions, the ability to enjoy every minute of life, to be here and now, to receive moral satisfaction from all your actions (even from pain), the knowledge that this pain can be shared with a person close in spirit, that this is an integral part of life.

The spiritual meaning of life can be called the most important, because it is without it that the material component quickly loses its value. This is the ability to withstand all the difficulties and troubles in life, to change, to benefit the world, to develop, to become stronger and wiser with every painful situation and crisis. Also, a significant part of the spiritual meaning is serving and helping people. On average, it is important for 99% of people to be useful to society. It is important not only to enjoy your actions, you need someone to notice, for someone it was useful, enjoyable, interesting.

Thus, people feel better, it inspires and makes you move on. The spiritual path can be not only external, but also internal, but in any case, a person feels how he is growing and getting better. From this point of view, without spiritual and emotional meanings there will be no material satisfaction, and vice versa. All this is closely interconnected, so you need to perceive the meaning of existence as an integral 3D picture.

In general, if we talk about the meaning of life, for many people it's life itself, the enjoyment of every minute lived, the process of work and dedication, the improvement of one's spiritual qualities, the ability to withstand difficult life's trials and emotional stresses (crazy joy, grief, difficult experiences), constant personal and professional development.

How to understand the meaning of your life? Everything is simple - you need to understand what a person enjoys from, this will fill his life with meaning.

How to understand that you feel sorry for yourself?

Moments of self-pity are characteristic of absolutely all people. For some, this is a "short pause" before moving forward to the intended goal, a kind of "rest" from the problems that have lumped in. For unsure personalities, this is an attempt, sometimes fruitless, to attract the attention and sympathy of the people around them.

What is the origin of such moments connected with?

How to understand whether a person pities himself?

There are three effective ways:

Observe your behavior - whether a person complains to close friends, family, acquaintances or people from a farther environment who are easier to complain about. This is the easiest way, but it requires some effort, because you have to admit that the problem really exists. How to do it?

In order to draw attention even to petty complaints, a negative attitude to life, to oneself and the successes of other people, it is enough to set oneself up, in which case any actions will be carefully analyzed by consciousness.

Ask yourself a frank question - do I have goals?

For example, a long-awaited and long-awaited marriage, a search for a loved one, a double increase in income, a strict diet and weight loss, a healthy lifestyle, etc. After that, it is necessary to analyze which of these goals have not been realized for a long time. The presence of unfulfilled tasks is an indicator that a person pities himself and does nothing.

Everything is simple - to fulfill any plan and project you need to at least start doing something. It is not difficult to take care of your health, but for this you need to get up from the couch and do exercises. To search for a loved one, you need to get acquainted and communicate with people, be open, etc. If a person does not move in anticipation of the fulfillment of his goals, then he pity himself.

To analyze whether there is an internal psychological stress in relation to the goal. In this case, it is better to choose a goal that is medium in duration, the most optimal option is a few weeks.

For example, the task was to follow a strict diet and not eat after 18.00. Several weeks passed, but nothing has changed - late snacks continue, the diet smoothly turns into the category of unrealized ideas, but at the same time, intense tension and self-criticism increase inside. This is evidence that a person pities himself.

So, there are 3 main indicators of self-pity:

- complaints out loud;

- unfulfilled dreams, "hanging" for a long time;

- internal tension in relation to desires and goals.

How to stop feeling sorry for yourself and continue to move forward?

First you need to realize that there is self-pity, then you need to work out and analyze the possible causes, develop further tactics of actions and firmly go to the intended goal.

How to find friends?

A topic that at first glance seems rather banal, is talked about, written and thought about. Of course, I don't want to try to compete with Dale Carnegie here, but I would like to share with you my observations from my personal life, from practical experience working with clients about what prevents us from making friends.

Recently, I have noticed more and more often that it has become difficult for many people, just to even call someone a friend. Somewhere in our unconscious, or perhaps even conscious, idea lives that in order to call someone else, he must be very, very verified, be a very, very old acquaintance and you can definitely trust him, because that he became very, very close to us. It seems that he should pass 3000 checks and only then, he can be called a friend. I do not agree with this idea, once getting rid of it, brought me three new friends, with whom I am still friends, and I am very glad about it.

But even if you do not want to get rid of this idea, this principle, but you are wondering: how to find a new friend and where should this friendship begin ?.

If you are a mature enough adult, then surely in your life the circle of friends and acquaintances is quite limited. Often the circle is limited to acquaintances, friends whom you meet at work, relatives and, possibly, those you meet with while attending some courses, gym, fitness and the like. But all this leads to the fact that we regularly see the same people, because it is rarely possible to meet a whole stream of new people who met in the life of an adult, mature person. And if you also work for yourself, not having a team of employees, then the circle narrows even more. And what is remarkable, if you observe a person who has been working in a team for several years, you will notice that he does not seek to make friends there, even if he is surrounded by many good people. At such moments, I wonder: why is this happening? And I come to the answer that people are simply afraid of pain, afraid of disappointment, afraid of resentment. It's simply afraid that the person whom they will consider their friend will betray them, deceive, disappoint. He will do something to hurt them ...

But, friends, is there any other way to check: is it possible to trust a person if you do not start to trust him?

So, I present to you a simple hacky life hack and at the same time homework.

Please recall all your surroundings, all the acquaintances whom you see at least occasionally: at work, at courses, in the gym, at fitness, perhaps in a cafe where you regularly have breakfast or dinner, in a bakery, etc. .d. And now choose among them the person who is most attractive to your soul. Not in terms of the fact that he looks attractive, but of the one who is most pleasant to you and with whom you would like to get close.

Next, the next point of this task - the next time you see this person, talk to him a little longer than usual. About anything: about the weather, about nature, about a common acquaintance, about some kind of event that happened. Sometimes you can ask how a person is doing. About what he thinks about this or that event, person, etc. Try to ask him one to three questions and develop a little conversation.

Repeat this another time, third, fourth. If you see that you are nice to this person, you feel that he is in contact with you, then once again, when you communicate with him, offer him a walk together, drink tea or go somewhere together. Of course, it would be desirable if you fall into the zone of interests of this person. Because, if you don't get it, then you can get a refusal not from the fact that he doesn't want to spend time with you, but because he is not interested in the action that you offer. Accordingly, offer so that the person understands that you are offering him just a joint pastime, just a joint leisure. In separate time from business.

For example, when I make such an offer to someone, I take and list: "Would you like / wouldn't like to drink tea together or take a walk, or go to some other place? Where the key word becomes: the word "together". I can repeat the word "together" several times, so that the person understands that I am not proposing a specific action, but simply spending time together. Believe me, in your environment there will be a man as bored as you are, and expecting someone to offer him a cup of tea, yearning for true friendship. Especially if you live in a big city, in a metropolis, because no matter how paradoxical it sounds, but the larger the city, the more lonely each of the inhabitants of this city.

Accordingly, take risks, do not be discouraged, look for your person, offer, and you will definitely find. The main thing - do not be afraid of pain and disappointment.

How not to be nervous when you are late?

To begin with, I would like to ask some questions for thought.

The first question is what is more important for you: you or the meeting you are late for?

You or a case that you do not have time to do?

What is more important for you: your health, your nerves, your peace of mind or the meeting you are late for?

And if you choose a meeting, then a very big question is why?

Why is your inner state not the most important thing in the world for you?

I understand, if it concerns a fateful meeting, when you are offered a job with a salary of two or three times more than you are used to. Or, when it comes to relocation or something else very global. But after all, most often our meetings are connected with everyday things and in fact, nothing global will happen if you are late for it.

Another verification question is: what will happen to you if you don't get to this meeting at all, or don't do this thing at all? What will change in your life?

What will become worse in your life?

I would like to open a small life hack for you.

The secret is simple: to call when you are late. Even if I'm late for five minutes, having warned the person who is waiting, I can give him the opportunity, for example, to have a snack, drink tea or just be distracted by something of my own. And it happens even the opposite happens, a person is grateful for these five minutes.

I understand that it can be a shame to do it, most likely you will feel guilty, you need to admit your guilt, it may be very difficult for you, but, in the end, most likely a person will respond normally to this call and you will feel much better.

The main thing is that you internally give yourself the right to be late. And here it is already important what tone you are talking to the person. If "Oh, because of the vi-ni-te, I am late," then such a tone will most likely cause your partner to whom you call, the reaction to scold you. And if you are confident enough, in a strong tone, say: "I'm sorry, I'm late, for 5-10 minutes - is this very critical?" A person will perceive you adequately. Of course, there are different situations when 5-10 minutes can really play a huge role, or at the time when you are half an hour late, an hour will be critical. At such moments, it's worth calling again and asking to postpone the meeting, because everyone can get into an unusual situation.

This life hack reminds me of an old Jewish joke that you may have heard too. When the husband and wife went to bed, and Abraham was spinning, spinning, panting, unable to sleep. Sarah asked him: "Abraham, what is it? Why aren't you sleeping? " He replies: "Yes, Moishe owes $ 500, I can't fall asleep." Sarah gets up, opens the window, shouts: "Moysha!" Moisha opens the window, shouting: "what, Sarah, do you want?" "Moysha owes you my Abraham 500 dollars?" "Yes". "So he won't give them to you." He closes the window, lays down in bed and says: "sleep, dear, let him not sleep now."

So in a situation of being late, in a sense it seems. Having warned a person, you have done your job and you can let go of your feelings. Of course, I didn't mean that now let the other person be nervous. Here is the moment to let go of the situation and calm down. But even if a person is nervous, what can you do, a similar situation can happen to everyone. In fact, all you have to do is reduce the importance of this meeting.

Because if you look globally at it, then in fact nothing terrible will happen. We actually treat many situations and many things in our lives much more anxiously and seriously than they would be worth it.

So ask yourself questions, call and allow yourself to be late.

How to deal with anxiety?

1.Keep a diary. It is advisable at the same time of the day, small deviations in time take place, but still try to adhere to the same time. Write everything down there. The next time I'll tell you about the diary, in a separate publication: how to keep it, what it is for, when it helps and that's it. I think it would be more logical to talk about him separately.

2. Walk regularly. Anxiety is very well removed by some rhythmic actions: regularly keep a diary, walk regularly. When you walk, stick to the same pace. If it's hard for you to self-discipline, get a dog. She will be your self-discipline. And you will walk regularly, in approximately the same rhythm.

3. Small physical activity. Periodically do exercises, go to the gym and so on. This can help stabilize the hormonal background of your body a little, help your body to get a little better.

4. You should have maximum control over what you can really control in your life.

5. Do not worry about the fact that you cannot control or change. I'll give you such a metaphor, I understand that perhaps some of you will disagree with me. But I believe that we cannot control our own weight, but we can control what we eat. Analyze what food affects us. For example, this food gives me more energy, I feel more cheerful, in good shape. And from this meal, I feel like I'm overweight and full. So you can control, but you cannot control the weight itself - this is the privilege of your body.

Or, for example, we cannot control whether another person will be late for our meeting. But you can take this risk into account and make a gap in your schedule. In fact, this world we can control only this way. That is, to do everything that is required of us, and to take into account that such or such an option can happen.

6. Do not worry about what did not happen. We are often in a hurry somewhere, and this state of hurry, often causes great anxiety, the very feeling that everything is running, running, running, you need to have time to do everything, do this and that, and it is like being on horseback all the time.

To be honest, I also experience similar situations, because I'm the same person as everyone, and sometimes I just stop myself, which I recommend to you. And I ask myself the question: is it so important to do this right today? What will happen to my life if I achieve this result in some business not now, but in a year? Well, given that I'm going to live up to 100 years at least, and I think that many of you also have enough life ahead, then what's the difference: will you do it today or will you do it in a month? Well, then why rush? But even if you know that your life is already limited, coming to an end, you still ask yourself the question: do you want to live the last days, months, years of your life quickly or with pleasure? Where are you in a hurry? After all, in the end, on your deathbed it will matter not so much to you how much you have done, but how much pleasure you have from life. Accordingly, do not forget to concentrate on pleasure, on here and now. Ask yourself all the time one question: what am I doing now and what am I feeling right now? It will bring you back to "here and now," and it will give you a feeling of greater fullness and greater enjoyment of life. And then you will not need to worry and rush to do everything in a hurry, if only as soon as possible.

How to get rid of chronic fatigue?

In the winter, for many, the topic of chronic fatigue becomes relevant. Of course, this condition can manifest itself at any time of the year, but in winter a person is much more at risk of overwork. What can be done with this fatigue, where to put it and how to get rid of it. I propose to talk about it!

There are two categories of causes that cause chronic fatigue:

1. The psychological category is stress, anxiety, too much workload, etc.

2. Physiologically objective - this is winter, lack of vitamins, poor sleep, poor nutrition, illness.

There is a lot to talk about the category, but I would like to draw your attention and give only one recommendation: now, indeed, many of us still have a winter period, now it is really much more difficult for the body to function, since there are almost no vitamins, sun and the like.

Our body has to draw resources from a kind of "generator", so spare yourself, do not force the body to work to the limit. Try during such a period, take maximum care of your health, do not set yourself tasks that are too complicated and require maximum effort.

I would generally recommend not setting global plans for the winter season. For me, the best plan for the winter period is the plan: to stay at least at the same level, not to leave, not to slide lower. It can be indicators at work, in personal relationships, etc., the main thing for me during this period is that it does not get worse. Do the minimum amount of work, the number of cases during the winter period.

And some projects and plans for the future, I always have a lot of them, I leave for the spring, summer. When there is more strength and energy, and now there is still a respite regime. If we talk about psychological difficulties, what to do, for example, in case of stress or overwork, there is only one answer to this - to rest in case of overwork and, as much as possible, to limit yourself as much as possible from stressful situations.

That sounds, of course, very simple. But I increasingly notice that many people do not know how to relax. Even when they are resting, for example, lying on the couch and watching TV or even going on vacation, they continue to scold themselves and think about work: I had to do this, and yet this and that, and that, and that ... Stop doing it. Give yourself the right to rest and give yourself the right to work. Define a schedule for yourself, write it down: at such and such a time I work, at such and such a time I am resting. The schedule will help you not to get confused about what to do and what not to do. Or maybe you even need to finally take a vacation.

Analyze: if you are a person who tends to scatter over a million things at once, then your task is to focus on one thing. At first it will be quite difficult to do, you will still be still busy with some second, third, twenty-fifth case, but it is important to understand that this is already a lot.

Try to limit your scope of affairs.

Find one of the most important, which will most of all advance you to your global goal.

This is the rule that I consider the most important: the human brain is not infinite, not rubber, it contains a certain amount of memory, a certain amount of perception and all other mental processes we have quite limited - this must be taken into account and taken into account.

We felt that you were full - rest, tired - rest. Everything else is not so important tasks, because in any case, it is better than if you get sick and do nothing at all.

Therefore, relax on time. Remember that you need a rest. And, if you are, on the contrary, a person who, as a rule, goes into one thing, plunges into it and completely forgets that you still have some other life - this is often characteristic of addicted people. In this case, please periodically emerge from your profession, from your hobby, from where you dive, and look around, what do you have besides your favorite business?

Remember about personal life, about hobbies, hobbies, friends and so on.

This is very important, because your psyche also gets tired when you are in contact all the time with only one thing. By the way, a lot of people abandon their profession precisely because they do not know how to dive in time, depending on their profession, they give it too much strength, energy and resources.

As a result, they are exhausted and believe that this is probably not theirs, they do not need it. But in fact, perhaps this is yours, but you just do not give yourself time to relax, forget about your right to rest.

So, I bring to your attention the basic four rules in order to avoid chronic fatigue and the consequences of this unpleasant condition.

1. This is a balance of work and rest. Find the regime in which you will be most effective, and such a regime is impossible without timely rest. Therefore, find this balance in your life.

2. Make up the structure of the day. Do it so that it is clear to you when, what, and how you are doing. Set yourself certain limits, determine how much you can do in a day. You know, your strengths, so cut back, do not let yourself be killed, do not kill yourself.

3. If you are resting, then please rest, and do not scold yourself: oh, how bad I am, that I am resting. You have the right to rest, you are the same person as all others.

4. If you feel very tired - take a vacation. Please give yourself the right to rest before your body takes this right for itself. Believe me, we are wonderfully arranged: when a person is too tired, he either gets very sick, at least with the flu, and at the maximum he can break his leg. Therefore, please prevent such things in advance. Sometimes or even often chronic fatigue is associated with increased anxiety. What to do with such anxiety, what to do if you "love" to engage in "self-flagellation", I will talk about this in one of the following articles. In the meantime, remember a simple rule: tired - relax!

How to quickly get out of depression?

Relatively speaking, depression can be divided into two main types: clinical and situational.

Clinical depression is one that can only be treated with medication, as well as with the help of psychotherapy, when you can't get out of this condition for a long time and, for example: lie on the bed for 2 years, you can't get up.

And there is a situational, calmer and minor form of depression, which appeared not so long ago. Here from it, you can quickly and effectively exit if you make your own efforts. Typically, such depression is associated with some situation. For example, not very good at work or in personal life.

We will talk about ways to get out of situational depression. Since clinical, already obliges the presence of a therapist in the treatment process.

First of all, in order to cope with situational depression, it is very important to identify for yourself what depression is associated with. It would be even better for you to hear and understand yourself, to understand what feelings were suppressed before the onset of depression. Depression is usually a suppressed feeling. And they are usually suppressed because of some kind of attitude, for example: you would like to feel anger at your beloved people, but the attitude is that you can't be angry with your beloved, I can't be angry with my husband, because I'm either angry on him, or love! Or anger at the parents, but then the form of depression is usually much deeper, because anger at the parents is formed over the long, long years, and accordingly, the wound has also formed over the long years.

Or for example, a feeling of tenderness may be suppressed. It would seem that such a good, warm feeling, but if my partner is not ready to accept this tenderness from me, and I have an attitude in my head that tenderness can be shown only to a person with whom I have a magical relationship.

That's it, I suppress this feeling of tenderness, I don't feel it for anyone, I don't show it, I don't give it away and accordingly it also causes depression. Another common installation option is a feeling of sadness. Sadness is a feeling that occurs when someone died or someone abandoned you, the relationship ended for some reason. Moreover, this happened a long time ago, but you still feel sad, the attitude comes again: "Well, how can you feel sad after 10 years? It is impossible! How can one be like that ?! " Starting to crush this feeling in yourself. And there are many such options, each can have its own version. In fact, depression is a feeling that should have manifested itself in you with great amplitude, and cover you with pain. But, of course, the body does not want to experience such severe pain and begins to defend itself from it. The result of what becomes depression ... The body reduces the amplitude of the pain, and it can stretch for a long - long time. Since it was not possible to fully live this pain right away. So, let's move on to 5 ways to quickly get rid of depression. I emphasize once again that this is precisely about situational depression.

1. A fairly effective and simple way is the method of switching. If you have depression associated with work - switch to a personal relationship, fall in love, go on a date ... In general, falling in love is fine, if you succeed, then depression will be removed by hand and for a long time.

2. The second way is to get creative. You can do ordinary things, but with a creative touch, for example, to wash dishes not with your right hand, but with your left hand, or clean the house in some other way, go to work using an unusual route for you. Or start drawing, writing, reading, reading involves imagination, and this is also a creative process. In general, whatever you do, attach some creativity, some spark of energy, this IGO, because depression, in fact, is a suppressed IG, a suppressed energy. Turn on the energy in some kind of creative process, hobby, allow yourself - dancing, singing, anything, do it several times, maybe this way it will become easier for you.

3. The third option is to change the type of habitual activity. For example, if you have sedentary or mental work, then be sure to engage in physical activity. Gym, jogging, yoga, or just do some exercises in the morning at home, choose what you like and do regularly. Thanks to a change of activity, the body includes new resources for you. If on the contrary, your work is associated with physical activity, then read a book, go to courses or training, give chewing gum to your mind.

4. The fourth option is to cry. If you want to cry, be sure to cry, the more you cry, the more this depression will come out through tears, yes, there is some sense in it. I understand that many of you have been set to cry, well - well - well, strong people do not cry! But sometimes crying is much better than if you keep strong. This will result in even greater weakness than if you now allow yourself a slight weakness. Especially men, men were forbidden to cry from childhood, men don't cry, trees die standing ... Men, you have the right to cry, cry, cry as much as you need. It is very good if there are relatives close by who support you, they will be nearby. If you cannot with your loved ones, cry at least one, alone

with yourself, this is very important, it also awakens new resources in our soul!

5. Well, the fifth option is to shout and curse. Find a safe environment where you can swear, a safe person, you can go out into the field and swear, you can make loud music and scream. You can beat the pillow with your hands, this is to the category of physical ones. Indeed, in such situations, anger is clearly hidden behind this depression. Let your body splash it out. You can sing, this is also a great way to shout out depression. Even if you don't know how to sing, sing if you want to. Like children, you know, they scream and they feel good. So you need it too, our inner children haven't gone anywhere, they are with us, with us all the time, so give yourself the freedom to do what you want.

   You can combine these methods, choose one that is most suitable for you, or use all five, and see what happens. Perhaps using these methods you will find your own method, one that will help you to cope with depression. Well, of course, remember that you can always turn to a specialist for help if you can't cope on your own.

How to stop being a victim?

And when he faces such pain, he has a poor alternative - either to experience it, or to do something with it. Sometimes it is so unbearable that a person ceases to feel it, but at the same time, it automatically ceases to feel all other feelings - love, joy, affection. Total anesthesia that destroys the living.

Further victimization takes place. Paradox - not wanting to experience the pain of violence, a person becomes a professional victim. How does this happen?

Having lost sensitivity, a person ceases to notice aggression directed against him. A person does not notice what is happening in contact with other people, and he has no way to deal with excitement and anger. Therefore, he continues to perform actions that provoke a situation of injury. Thus, a victim of sexual violence can organize his life in such a way as to be in a situation of a threat of recurrence of such violence. Or the victim of emotional violence surrounds himself with people who are able to constantly "force" her emotionally. Or the victim of physical violence behaves in a way that provokes a fight. And he does it in the company of people easily excitable for physical aggression. And the choice is always accurate! Around the victims there is always a circle of people organizing a repeated injury to him.

How to change this?

It's never too late to start worrying.

If repeated cases of violence happen and happen in your life, it is very important to notice that what happens in contact with other people is abnormal. It happens that a person tells the story of his life in a monotonous calm voice, and another's blood runs cold in his veins and his hair stands on end. And often the sensitivity of the trauma is restored by other people who will tell him that this is not normal. But the consequences of the restored sensitivity are a strong flurry of emotions that will appear here. This is buried pain, anger and anger - and it is important to deal with them.

It is normal to experience pain, anger and shame, but another person is important, next to whom you can do it. After all, without experiencing feelings, there is a big threat of their repeated encapsulation and return to normal.

It is also important to find a way to make contact in a different way, slowly getting rid of the role of the victim. For example, to notice that in contact with a person you have a real desire to say "no" - and move on to this reaction.

The more you try to take new actions in relationships with other people, the more chances you will go beyond victimization.

How to deal with unpleasant feelings?

Stage 1

Notice the feeling that torments you. Paradoxically, sometimes it is not possible to identify the feeling. Sometimes you know that shame, guilt, or anger interferes with you, and sometimes you don't even notice it. You simply replace the feeling with some action, for example, beat dishes so as not to feel angry. Or experience insomnia so as not to feel anxiety. If the feeling is painful and strong, it is easier to block it than to face it. The first stage is extremely important because, having lost sensitivity and not understanding what is happening to you, you will very soon lose your taste for life.

Stage 2

When you notice an unpleasant feeling, it will seem to you that the quality of your life has worsened. Now all this needs to be handled. Previously, you did not feel shame or simply did not make contact with other people in order not to know about it. Previously, you were not tormented by feelings of guilt, but simply constantly doing something. Therefore, the second important stage is the legalization of feelings - to give him the opportunity to stay and live in you. Any feeling has the right to life and is legal. Any feeling fulfills a certain function, feelings heal. They are designed to change your life for the better, so it is important to give it the opportunity to exist, in spite of the fact that you want to run away from awareness and very quickly.

Stage 3

At the moment when you are aware of a feeling, do not run away from it and legalize it; it is important to look around and see if there are people nearby with whom you would like to share this feeling, having told about it. Most likely, you will understand that you are scared or unpleasant to talk about feeling, but deep down you will notice a signal that telling you is still important. This is not the case when it is better. If you went through two stages, it is important to move on. Try to find people with whom you would like to share this. Here you need what is called. This is when you talk about feeling to someone in person, looking in the eyes. And notice what happens to you when you talk about your feeling. Here is a place where all miracles can happen. It's not even important what you say about feeling, but how you feel about it. After all, speaking of fear, you can at the same time notice gratitude to the other person who is listening to you, or self-confidence.

This is a key necessary step.

Speaking of fear, you may begin to notice a feeling that you are stronger than you thought, or a feeling of joy. To notice something new that lies against the background of toxic feelings is a very important point that you can begin to experience bodily. In this place you need to be as attentive as possible. The emergence of something new in contact will constantly transform you and your feelings. For example, you may notice that your gratitude has become more than fear. So, step by step, you will have a new option - not only to feel something else, but also to do something in a new way. Freedom of action and the ability to manage contact. For example, shame paralyzed you before, and now you can communicate and ask questions. Ask if people think about you what you think they think. At that moment you get the feeling that it is you who are the center of your life. And you can control it. To manage does not mean to control, but to notice and manage so that it is comfortable and useful for you.

How to understand what is behind desires?

What is the difference between desires and needs? Are these concepts equal?

Desire is the materialization of needs, their objectification. Needs themselves are not material, but they feed on what we get in the material world. In other words, desire is a kind of "I want," and need is a "I eat." How do I know if I'm getting what I want?

There are no direct signs that you are eating. In each case, you need to understand.

For example, you want to earn a lot of money to buy whatever you want. There is no need for money, but money can satisfy the need for security, recognition, acceptance, and even love. The only question is how much money is needed for you to eat. If you earn, earn and this is the meaning of your life, but deep down you remain hungry, that means you missed with need. The need for recognition, love and acceptance is not met by money. What if you want and receive, but remain unfilled?

This is the main problem. Since a priori desires are not equal, moreover, they are often borrowed on Instagram, you can run about your "want" for a century, but stay with nothing.

For example, if your need for love and intimacy, then you are not satisfied with many sexual relationships.

If your need for security, then buying an iPhone, you also do not decide anything.

If your need for recognition, then even the highest performance indicators in the library will not satisfy you. And branded clothing may not help either. And the latest Mercedes model too. Need to look for other options.

If, after satisfying a desire, you feel rather empty than full, then with desire you have missed. How to sort it out?

Feel like a surgeon of your own psyche. Pay attention to yourself.

 In your life, by all means, there is some kind of, conditionally, let's say a symptom that tells you that somewhere you are not doing that.

Are you satisfied every day?

Yes?

Do you want to go home in the evening and work in the morning?

There may be hundreds of such questions, ask yourself. Something in life you definitely don't like. Pay attention to this. What is it? Work, friends, inability to say no, not enough joy?

Delve into this - when is this dissatisfaction, this symptom, do you have it?

When do you find yourself not quite at odds with happiness?

Maybe this happens after talking with some people?

Maybe when you do not get attention?

Who are these situations related to?

Could it be that your symptom is associated with a specific person?

Who is this person?

How can he help you with this?

Can you ask him about it?

Rely, if you like, on the scheme of studying yourself - what is happening now? - what does it cause? - what feelings do I have? - which person or group of people is involved in this? - how can I help myself?

Most of the problems in our lives arise because we do not know our needs. And without realizing the needs, we form desires with a downed scope. We can satisfy the need for smuggling like children.

For example, we want attention, and cause a scandal. We want cares and begin to hurt. We want love and make money. There are hundreds of situations, there are thousands of examples, but only you can understand what is inside you, where you slip yourself and what you do not notice. And most often - in contact with other people.

Each person inside has, conditionally, a lottery drum, the needs of which are balls. And every time in contact with people some balls appear on the surface - you notice them. And each time one of the balls turns out to be more empty than others - in this place you are starving more. This is a figure.

Relatively speaking, if you want to eat candy, then eating cottage cheese, salad, fish and meat you will not stop wanting candy. So it is with demand balls - if your need for recognition is starving more than the need for security, without sitting at home under the covers, you will not fill this need with anything.

Unconscious needs have the greatest impact on a person. All your actions, all the choices you make, all the steps in life are connected with needs and their embodiment - desires.

The greatest happiness is to combine needs and desires, but this is not easy to do. This is the way and study of yourself. This is attention to oneself. This is contact with other people. This is the life for which you take responsibility. And that, not a deficit. This is life to the fullest. And a little clue. Need is affirmation. If you do not want something, it is not a need or desire. Look for what you want and what you eat.

How to be full?

What is psychological satiety?

What is the philosophy of excess and deficit talking about?

How to turn hunger into satiety, and deficiency in excess?

When it comes to the philosophy of deficit, it is understood that inside a person does not, relatively speaking, have an organ that is responsible for satisfaction.

When, for example, a woman who considers herself unclaimed by men receives a compliment that she is beautiful, these words pass by her.

The tragedy of the situation is that no matter how much she receives compliments, recognition and satisfaction, she will never be full. This is hunger and the philosophy of scarcity.

The philosophy of scarcity is always based on the feeling that resources are scarce. In the outside world there can be a huge number of them, but satisfaction does not come.

People with such a philosophy live in the feeling that something else needs to be done to get even more. So most families who seek therapy in a crisis are 80-90 percent in one similar situation - something is different from each other require.

One, for example, wants love and recognition, and the other wants tenderness and care. Then the task is to demand from the other that which he himself lacks. And now two people sit hungry, negotiate with each other, set conditions and ultimatums. It is touching, sad and without options. As long as one of the partners expects that what he lacks will give the other, and then he will think about giving something in return, nothing happens. This is a dead end.

There is an idea that the amount of resources in the world is limited, and the task is to get them, keep them in yourself and only then share them with someone else. Theoretically, this is true. But this is true, received, perhaps, in childhood. After all, a person who has not received love and has not eaten since childhood, is not able to give this love. In adulthood, its own truth. It lies in the fact that from the philosophy of scarcity to the philosophy of excess, you can go.

This can be done by realizing a simple thing - all resources are inside. Magic happens when you go from hunger to a state of excess, finding inside what you want to share. When the question is not "how do I get what I want from a partner," but "what would I like to say or give to my partner."

The moment you start loving another for yourself, you will find that the amount of energy in your life is increasing. The more you spend for yourself personally, the more you get. But understanding what exactly you do is important here.

If you do charity work to make other unhappy people happier, this will not work. To do for yourself is to do charity work, because you personally enjoy watching how happiness becomes greater in life.

An even more radical example is the parent. Mothers often love their children so that the children feel good. Parents often give their children everything they can, and they themselves are waiting for some better future to eat, for example, a delicious cake that only children can get now. This is a bear service. Children then cease to be satisfied. All cakes given by parents pass through the child's transit. For the formation of a healthy child, healthy parents who also want cakes are important. Who generally want something for themselves, and not for the child. The best mother is happy. When a mother employs an assistant or nanny for her baby, that's good. Because the mother then ceases to be a victim. The story of

Danko, who tore his heart out to illuminate the world, deforms the relationships of other people. Heroic deeds are justified in other situations.

In today's world, heroism is not in demand. Contractual, honest, good relations are demanded in which all participants are comfortable. And also satiety and excess are in demand, which I want to share.

It is important to realize what you would like to give the world. What would you like to share with people. What do you have that would be useful to other people. What you have so much that it's impossible to keep in yourself.

If you want to write poetry not so that people applaud, but because you want to do it personally, or if you want to give love to other people, because you have this love, this is an excess. And such an excess is selfish.

Be selfish. It works in all areas of life. There is nothing wrong with egoism, and the philosophy of excess is the philosophy of rich people. And this helps to develop psychotherapy. Come to become rich and well fed

How to decide on a change in life?

Are there ways to alleviate anxiety and fear of change? This question most often worries people who are on the verge of change, or even change something in their lives, but are worried. There is no answer to it.

It is impossible to get rid of the anxiety associated with change, and take risks at the same time. If you dare to change something in your life, this does not mean that all the people around you will support you and say that you are well done.

Fear is a necessary companion to any change. And the scope of this fear is directly proportional to the significance and radicalism of these changes. The more you want to change in your life, the stronger will be the fear. If you have lived your life in the same conditions, worked in the same place, despite the fact that you do not like it, the very idea that you can no longer work there causes you great fear. If your whole life you have relied on the rules that your parents or other authorities created for you, and you want to change something in these beliefs, fear will invariably accompany this. Fear is also what naturally stops us from changing. Culture came up with this as a kind of regulatory mechanism.

If someone could guarantee that we will change our activities and become a free artist, we will not starve to death and be successful, of course, we would say "yes" and go to it. But then the value of the changes would be minimal. You can never predict the effectiveness of your changes and the outcome. Moreover, with significant changes, your entire environment will mind. The reasons are obvious - the people around you, especially close ones, are used to this. They do not want to see you others. They do not think about values and other aspects of your changes; they want stability for themselves. And this is normal.

If you change jobs, your family is involved. And for everything there is a price. On the one hand, you refuse what is painful for you and prospects open up before you, but no guarantees. There are many fears. Therefore, often, in order to decide on changes, you either need to get to the pen and physically feel bad, or you need significant support from the outside.

If you get support and acceptance from significant people even in case of failure, your fear will not become less. He will become enduring.

The question is not to get rid of fear, but to balance it. What can balance fear? A strong craving. Faith in you of other people and the ability to rely on someone. It is likely that you will not be taken back from work, but your fear will be balanced by the support you receive.

Moreover, if you try to get guarantees, most of your passion and desire to change something will go into these guarantees. The value of change will not be so great. If the fear is insignificant, you simply do not appropriate all the changes that have occurred.

Be mindful of fear. He is important. If you are afraid, you want what you fear. This is a litmus.

How to be effective in everything we do?

If the activity is in the zone of the figure, we will be effective. If we try to implement tasks that are in the background, then we will not be effective. Because the figure still comes out on top and eats up what we do.

So, for example, if we quarreled with a loved one, all our thoughts are in this place. Our need for love, recognition, respect and relationships is key. We can return ourselves to work as much as we like and force ourselves to think about it, but there will be no efficiency. Because we do not live in the process of work, now we live in a relationship.

Do not be fooled. If you do something that does not fit your needs, you lose. It remains to understand where the needs come from and what they are?

Most of our needs are conceptual. This is what we spied on by other people. This is what coaches and authors of success books exploit. Ideas about what a happy life should be are passed from head to head.

The problem is that we may not need what someone else has, but there is another need that responds with envy. For example, there is a need for recognition, and we envy the author of a book that has become popular. This does not mean that you need to write a book without feeling any buzz from the writing process. But you can make a great show, give a good lecture, or make a cool movie.

The most important thing is to ask yourself the question "what do I want", and not "what needs to be done to get what I envy."

Only by realizing our needs, we can understand the desire - to withdraw our figure, where the most energy. Then the activity will bring fullness, a sense of life and buzz. And this is the only way to check whether our desire is real, or peeped. And here there are difficulties.

First, we will never know for sure whether our desire really belongs to us. In the case of real energy, we will always be overcome by doubts. After all, energy is what I want, and not what is right. And since we do not know whether what we are doing is right, we cannot get rid of doubts either.

The second - we do not predict how long this desire will be relevant. It can be full of energy day, week or year. The figure may not be relevant forever and certainly not for life, as success coaches say, advising you to set a goal, create a dream and go to it. The figure is changing. So some needs are ahead of others and require our attention elsewhere.

So our effectiveness ranges from whether we are returning ourselves to our intended goal, or truly understand what we need. Listening to ourselves, asking ourselves questions and realizing our figure and background, we come closer to what is the efficiency, energy and success of what we do.

But this path is much more complicated than following someone else's success. And the easiest way to go this path in the program of psychotherapy.

How to find yourself?

The good news is that no one was lost. You have always been yourself, you just don't really like your opinion about yourself today. It's not that you lost yourself, but that you don't know what you are. We are used to living in a world in which we are all trying to change. And the big illusion is that we are changing ourselves. But our self-image does not change, it summarizes. The experience of the past years of life, which makes us look at ourselves differently, is constantly being added to us. We never stop being children.

We are what we are. But to our yesterday we add today's. How does this happen? In our programs and personal therapy, people often pursue insights - some insights about the motives of their actions and actions. And they can be quite strong and vibrant. But in fact, small remarks about the new ones work differently - more efficiently. Small, not very significant reactions, new feelings and thoughts, not necessarily bright and transforming, can have a greater impact on you than what you are striving for. The number and strength of insights has nothing to do with the effectiveness of psychotherapy. Small observations and tiny changes also lead to what is called finding oneself. The phrase itself would be worth replacing with another - to grow oneself out of oneself.

You become a high-class professional when this professional grows from within you. All that is needed is to enable you to become who you are. After all, what is the danger to spy on people's lives?

The fact that you can feel like an imposter all your life. The one you found with advice, books or observations may be some other person other than you. Not by you. And you will spend strength and energy to become one.

Give yourself the opportunity yesterday to add to yourself today. Then you will notice that the one you were looking for was always with you.

How to be present in your own life?

Quite often there are situations when we are bodily present in one place, and our life is in another. Our life at this moment may be in some kind of illusions, dreams or worries about what we did not do today, in reflection on the problems that were yesterday or those that need to be addressed.

There are frequent situations when people talk with each other and are distracted all the time, sometimes during a 2-hour conversation, not even a minute being present at the place of conversation.

The luxury of psychotherapy is that a space is created in which two people can simply be present, touching each other's lives.

Imagine that only by letting your life touch the life of another person, you gain access to unlimited changes as if you are entering a different world and a different reality.

In quantum mechanics there is the concept of coupled states. This is the same condition that we access by being present. Every second, our brain receives millions of bits of information, and is able to process only two thousand. Our perception is so narrowed that we are able to catch only a small part of the world. To a large extent, this is because we use concepts to connect with other people. The more hypotheses and projections we have regarding another person, the less we change. How technically is the presence?

Imagine a person with whom you would like to spend more time at the level of the heart. Suppose this is a close person who is waiting for you at home. Try to meet him, sit opposite each other. Look at him and listen to yourself. Now your life is directly connected with the life of this person. And inside you have some reactions that you have never noticed before, or those that fill your heart. Now try to say about these reactions to a person as if there is no one else on this earth. Personally to yourself, personally to another. Try to listen to what you want to say to the person, and say it. And notice what happens to you when you say that. Then this person listens to himself and his reactions, which appeared in contact with you. And he says it to you. To myself, to you personally. You will notice how strong an energy effect can come from this exercise. But nothing is easier than that. Nothing is simpler and nothing more difficult. You will notice how difficult it will be for you to communicate this way, because it is very unusual. You will notice that you will want to not only tell your person about your condition to this person, but explain, ridicule, and ironic. This will indicate that an excess of arousal that you cannot bring into contact will force you to leave it.

Stop. Listen to yourself again. You can also notice embarrassment, shame, awkwardness, fear, and suddenly a person does not understand or will run away from contact. Opening up to another person, we can get hurt. In the ordinary world, we are protected by concepts, therefore we run and do not stop, and it is difficult to reach us. At the moment of presence, we are open. And just then a miracle happens.

A miracle is that which should not be, but it is. This thought should not have appeared, but it has appeared. So it is with feelings that should not be in contact with a wife, daughter, for example. And it appears.

It is so impressive that it can change the world. And perhaps this is only in the act of presence.

How to become happy and rich?

Currently, a whole movement of successologists - people who help others to acquire the necessary skills to achieve success in their lives - has appeared in psychological practice. Trainings are held in different cities, gathering up to several hundred participants - "The main secret of success" or "How to make a million", "How to attract money into your life" or "How to get married successfully".

According to my observations, however, most often real success and careful preparation for it are alternatives. People who make money, and those who go to trainings to make money, are often very different people.

Women who learn how to get married and women who are happy in the family are also different people. Vainly planning to have children and not being able to get pregnant women, on the one hand, and happy mothers who do not think about it, are also not the same people.

And finally, therapists trying to build their practice with the effort of thought and will, and therapists with rich private practice are also different people. Why is this so? And does this mean that efforts should not be made to achieve what is desired?

I will try to answer these questions. I will rely on the ideas of field dynamics, which are characteristic of the dialog-phenomenological approach in psychotherapy. Let me remind you that, according to the ideas about the field that exist within the framework of this approach, field dynamics is governed by concepts and experiences. These are two forces that define our whole life. Moreover, clear and stable external criteria for these two processes do not exist.

They can be phenomenologically very similar. The difference is rooted only in their nature. The same phenomenological context and even the same phenomenological chain can be inscribed in both the concept and the experience. The point is not in the content of the process of life, but in its quality.

Turning to our current topic, this means the following. You can realize your conceptual dream of children, doing everything possible and almost impossible for this, and without having obvious or implicit difficulties of a medical nature, not get pregnant.

Or you can just want children, experiencing it with all your heart and get pregnant the first time. You can have a concept that outwardly can be completely indistinguishable from the desire to get married and desperately "kill" against the harsh walls of "real life". And you can experience this desire for closeness and care, and, as a rule, a man immediately appears.

The difference is in the nuances of field dynamics, and not in the content of the "dream". Most often, in training to achieve anything, all the efforts of the facilitator and, accordingly, of the participants are focused on processing the concept. As a rule, participants in such trainings are carriers of the corresponding dream concept.

Therefore, it does not matter whether we visualize our dream or break down the process of its achievement into stages, this will not help. Moreover, the corresponding concept is likely to intensify. And since she is an agent of the self-paradigm, this process will lead to the consolidation of her vicious circle. The collapse of primary experience occurs in the usual way - the "dream", as before, remains unattainable.

In terms of the cone-layer model of the field, this means that you and I move along a particular conceptual layer of the self-paradigm that the corresponding dream-concept has at its disposal. So here is the "train", pushed by strong-willed efforts, and moves in a circle around the base of the cone. What is the alternative? I believe it is already obvious to you, dear reader. Since the primary experience is located at the top of the field cone, any psychological transformations are possible only when moving in this direction. And the only transport that can deliver us there is experience.

Therefore, the alternative that dialog-phenomenological psychotherapy offers is to accompany this force field vector. However, we know that we cannot directly control the experience - we can only surrender to it.

Therefore, if a client has applied for psychotherapy about difficulties in realizing one or another conceptual "desire", this does not mean at all that in the process of experiencing it it will remain for a long time. Perhaps it is only marked some aspect of the blocked experience, restoring which, the need for it simply disappeared as unnecessary.

How to deal with unpleasant colleagues - whiners, liars, aggressors?

1. Idealization. At the stage of adaptation to a new place of work, there is a lot of anxiety and romantic love. Akin to human love, when we do not notice any shortcomings, but exalt our beloved on a pedestal. And suddenly, colleagues begin to treat you aggressively. You think what is connected, it is with you, but the reasons may be different. For example: your salary is higher than that of colleagues because you sold yourself better and salaries are assigned randomly in the company. Last come - received more. You took the place of the favorite of the team and involuntarily involuntarily everything that you do falls under the microscope. The boss is inclined to create special conditions for beginners - to excessively and undeservedly praise in the team. There is such a myth - that everyone should treat each other well. This is something that seems to be taken for granted. But in this myth, two bottlenecks are "must" and "good." Why should you be treated well? You are not godfather, matchmaker, brother? And what does "good" mean? Do not scold, do not demand !? What you need to clearly enough understand that getting into a new team, we join in the competition. For resources - money, attention, toilet paper, oxygen. And if you do not take money from a colleague, then you are definitely absorbing part of the oxygen. That already at an unconscious level can provoke aggressive behavior. And the battle for the on and off air conditioning. Here is an enemy out of the blue. You are hot and cold. And you need to agree.

2. Victim behavior. I am far from the idea that the reader, these lines is an angel. They are in heaven, and people on earth. Therefore, the story that everyone offends me, I can not tell you the poor and unhappy. This is one side of the coin. The other side is that I am confident that you have done something so that your neighbor comes up and decides to kick you in the kneecap, and then do it all the time with increasing pleasure. You are not a sheep, and the aggressor is not a wolf. Each of you is a person trained to protect your personal boundaries and space. For example, comes in, someone takes a personal notebook to you and starts flipping through. Your jaw dropped, your eyes express amazement, but you don't have enough strength to express your feelings. As a child, Toli, my mother, said that to fight badly and everything should be common, either he is big and strong, and you are small and weak. In this seemingly innocent scene, there is a lot of violence. The aggressor found the victim and launched the first test ball.

Further, the situation can unwind in a spiral with a larger amplitude. A whiner, contrary to the conventional wisdom of opinion, is not a victim at all. This is also the manipulator and the aggressor. Under the guise of an offended virtue and with righteous anger on your lips, it will sit opposite you and begin to talk about how the world is unfair to him, to you, which goats and fools are around. And you are a special person who understands. I met people who with the help of such manipulation easily survived people from the team. I mean, it is important to allow such an opportunity inside yourself that aggressive behavior, deception, etc. troubles provoked and you including. Especially if this situation is not one-time, but permanent. Remember that the Aggressor is primarily a Coward. He is afraid that he will be offended, so he attacks the first. Inside, this is a fragile and unhappy person. Just keep that in mind in the background. Its main motive is safety. The poor thing is very, very scared to him.

3. Psychopaths among us. If you look at the International Classification of Diseases of the 10th revision, you will see how many mentally ill people are among us. Three five per hundred. Often, people with psychopathy hold leadership positions and are business owners. It was they in the 90s who were able to overcome everything that lies badly. Psychopathy is a psychopathological syndrome that manifests itself in the form of a constellation of traits such as heartlessness in relation to others, a reduced ability to empathize, an inability to sincerely repent of harming other people, lying, self-centeredness, and superficial emotional reactions. If fate has made you sick and upset with a sick person, it's useless. It's like a manifestation of the weather - rain, wind, snow. They may not like it, but they are taken by us for granted. Psychopaths are great manipulators. A textbook example is the Milady of the Three Musketeers. See how skillfully she spun her whole environment. Upstream and downstream. To win it took the participation of four men. Rate your strength. Are you ready to deal with the painful manifestations of another person. Listen to intuition. If not, leave. It will be cheaper.

4. Techniques to resist manipulation. Take the initiative in your own hands. Set boundaries. You have every right to tell another person. Say the facts that you observe: "You speak very loudly, in a raised tone. Are you angry Let's talk in peace. " Way out of the situation: "I'm busy now." Speaking of feelings: "I don't like what you say. I do not want to communicate with you in a similar manner. " You should understand what the interlocutor means. Clear out all the fuzziness and bottlenecks. The introduction of the regulation: "I have two minutes, after which I need to leave." The formula for stopping the manipulation of social

psychologist Philip Zimbardo, which you should first say to yourself for awareness, and then say to another: "I can continue to live without your love, friendship, disposition, abuse, even if such an action can hurt - until you stop doing X and you won't start doing Y. "

Freedom is when the freedom of one rests on the freedom of another and has this last condition. So, if you have or in the mouth after communication an unpleasant aftertaste appears, it was a manipulation. Freedom is, above all, freedom of choice. In most situations, it is present in our lives, but to use it you need to learn to separate reality from illusions.

How to improve the relationship between spouses?

There is a saying: "every unhappy family is unhappy in its own way, and all happy families are equally happy" - I completely agree with this statement.

Happy relationships are built on intimacy, trust and honesty between partners who are destroyed in unhappy relationships due to the use of so-called power games, such as, for example, lodges. These games are well and very clearly described by Claude Steiner in his book "The Other Side of Power."

An important signal of the presence of games in your family is that one of the spouses does not have autonomy from the other: household, financial, psychological.

For example, a wife does not work or earns less than she spends on herself, that is, in the event of a breakdown with her spouse, she cannot leave the relationship and continue to provide for herself. In this case, the first thing she needs to do is to become financially independent from her spouse, because in the process of working with games, if her partner is not interested in giving up games, for example, is not interested in giving up lies and betrayals, then her decision giving up games will lead to her desire to get out of a relationship with such a man, and this, in turn, will lead her to an internal conflict with her financial dependence on her spouse.

When working with power games in your family, the first thing to do is start to notice when you are in the game and what kind of game it is.

Most often, the games between the spouses concern joint issues, such as sex, love, the choice of a place for joint vacation, the issues of arranging a joint life, and so on.

Further, as soon as you see the games that you play with your spouse, you can use the antithesis to the game you found: that is, the ways to exit the game are from Claude Steiner's book mentioned above.

However, I repeat, it must be borne in mind that if your partner is not interested in quitting games, then your attempts to apply the antithesis to games can lead to a break in your relationship - you need to be prepared for this.

In addition to analyzing games, you also need to practice relationships of closeness and trust with a partner - for this, joint projects where you act together as a team, such as a joint trip to the mountains, organizing your own wedding, paired body and energy practices, giving birth to a child and etc.

However, if we talk about the birth of a child, I do not recommend using it to try to solve the problems that have matured in a couple, since the child will not solve them, but will only aggravate and reveal new games and conflicts between you that you were not previously aware of.

Therefore, it is worth deciding on the birth of a child only if you have already solved the conflicts and games that you already see in your couple.

How to increase your sex appeal?

Mostly women turn to me with a request to work with sexuality, to increase their sexual attractiveness, so I will talk specifically about female sexuality.

Sexual attractiveness leads to a greater interest in men in you, that is, a greater choice of a potential partner, however, it does not guarantee success in a long relationship with a man, since sexuality alone is not enough for such a relationship.

There is a widespread belief that a woman is made sexy by large breasts, full lips, a thin waist, and so on.

In my opinion, this opinion is erroneous, since it contradicts the observed facts: there are many successful men and sexually attractive women from the male point of view, about whom we can say that they are "chubby", "with small breasts" and with other "shortcomings", and at the same time next to them you can see women with figures much more "correct" from the point of view of the opinion described above, but deprived of male attention.

For example, in the fitness room you can often notice that a chubby woman on training machines is sexually more attractive than her trainer with an "ideal" figure.

For example, I can say that the same common opinion about men is the fallacy that women are sexually attracted to pitching, although I think most of you women agree with me that this is not so.

In fact, both men and women are sexually attractive by their high level of energy, which is read by us at a subconscious level, and then rationalized by consciousness: she has this and that and that's why she and I are attracted to others, but nearby stand a woman with very similar external data, but she will not attract the attention of this man if she has a low level of energy (he most likely will not even notice her as a woman).

For men and women, a high level of energy is manifested as dignity, self-confidence, self-esteem, and besides this for men it is charisma when he is passionately involved in some business, outward orientation (extravert), giving, and for women like relaxation, full acceptance, openness, orientation inward (introversion).

Since we have everything: the body, psyche, energy are connected, we can work on the same task from different angles, including at the same time to enhance the positive effect.

To increase sexual attractiveness through the body, it is necessary to understand that the more relaxed and open a woman is, the more sexual she is. That is, to increase your sexuality, first of all, you need to move in the direction of relaxation of your body.

The main criterion by which you can determine whether your body is tense or not is the tension on your face. If your face is tense, then your body is also tense.

A striking example of such a tension is compressed lips, a woman with compressed lips for most men will be less sexually attractive than the same woman, but with relaxed facial muscles and a relaxed mouth. This is one of the reasons why many men are attracted to women in or after the sauna: because the sauna helps the woman relax as much as possible and become the most host.

If your body is tense, then you need to help it relax, for example, you can go for a relax massage, yoga, dance, aerobic exercise in the fitness room or in the sauna.

Any body care procedures, such as going to the hairdresser, to the beautician, massage therapist, also help well.

However, it is important that someone else did these procedures for you, and not you yourself, since when you do some procedure yourself, you are faced with the task of doing everything correctly and this will not let you completely relax, turn off the control and start taking, and it's just relaxing and turning off control that is important to achieve from the procedures described above in the topic of increasing sexual attractiveness.

These can be "ordinary" and often inexpensive procedures, for example, an appeal to a hairdresser: and we are not talking about some beautiful hairstyles, hairstyles, etc. - you just came to cut your hair, combed you, paid attention, you relaxed and rested. You can even ask for a free service from a specialist who is studying or is just starting to practice and needs work for a portfolio.

Pair dances give a stronger effect in terms of increasing energy levels than individual ones: the more contact ones with a partner, the better, for example, cha-cha-cha, waltz, hustle, etc. The face is well relaxed with a gentle massage such as a brush massage on the face.

As for yoga, it's better, nevertheless, that yoga should not be in the fitness option, but in a specialized center where the trainers are more qualified and pay much attention to setting up the body in asanas, then the energy flows correctly and energy is taken.

But all these nuances and recommendations are important when you have already begun to study and you want to increase the effect of classes - but for most of my clients with such a request it is important to just start helping your body relax: in any way possible. After this procedure, you can notice the incredible effect of this "ordinary" service: men pay more attention, say compliments. And, perhaps, you will be wondering why it would be, you, like, did not change anything special in yourself, did not dress up, but only took care of yourself, gave yourself love and attention, and the men felt this and immediately reacted.

However, all these methods of relaxing the body will only give a temporary effect if you do not work with the psyche, since often the source of our tension is in the head: in the habit of negatively evaluating ourselves and others, in our closeness.

When working through the psyche, it is necessary to learn to leave the evaluative position in relation to oneself and others, especially men, and to show more acceptance, since evaluation and criticism, so characteristic of our women, lead to the fact that the body is pinched, closed and becomes asexual .

By the way, often fitness gives a positive effect, not only because aerobic exercise relaxes the body, strengthens our energy, but also because a woman ceases to worry and be shy about how she looks and becomes more relaxed and relaxed from this.

However, it often happens that we are unable to understand why our body is pinched again and again, it is not possible to independently determine the psychological causes that lead to this, and then we need the help of a specialist psychologist.

When working through bodily-energy practices, the same process occurs: in the first stages you relax the body: for example, through intense breathing, shaking, buzzing and other techniques - and then the stage of meditation begins, which puts you in a meditative state, a state outside of the ego, in which, by definition, there is complete acceptance and relaxation, where there is no evaluation, since evaluation is part of the ego.

In addition, the practices are aimed at strengthening the state of the "internal observer", which will help in determining the reasons why we strain and "drain" the energy between the practitioners, for example, identify people with whom we especially lose energy, and understand which it is the problem in us that these people use to later work out this problem in practice or with a psychologist.

I want to draw your attention to the fact that for lack of sexual attractiveness there is often a child's decision "not to be sexually attractive", which has its cause in the past and the result in the form of sexual unattractiveness in the present. That is, often behind the desire to be more sexually attractive is an internal conflict: one part of you may want this, and it is recognized by you, the other part may resist this and not be realized.

How to become more aware?

Awareness is not only the ability to reason your own actions, allowing the rational mind to triumph. Awareness is the acceptance of oneself as the creator and creator of one's experience, the insight into the very essence of all things and the awareness of the mechanism of creation. When the mechanism of creation becomes clear, creation becomes intentional and begins to bring pleasure.

Why is becoming more conscious - is it cool? Because from the chaotic, murky biomass that removes you from business and decides your fate in your office, the world around you turns into a mechanism governed by laws - laws that can be learned and used to create what you want, and not what something like that "happened.

There are four main steps for developing awareness:

To see the self-deception that a person is engaged in.

To realize that the world is a big mirror, where everything around us is our aspects that we project outward (and which, incidentally, it's time to put it back together).

To find out that everything that happens to you, you pulled to yourself to give yourself the opportunity to develop.

Consider rationality, orderliness and organization around you. Accept the paradox of creation.

The first three steps are practical.

The fourth step follows as a natural conclusion that a person makes himself based on the results found.

The main obstacles for developing awareness are closed thinking and the habit of shifting responsibility for decision-making to other people.

As long as thinking is closed, a person is in the paradigm of a rehearsed worldview. As taught, it does. For a person with a closed way of thinking, education ends after school. At best, after university. But you should not poke your finger at a person like a leper. To one degree or another, closed thinking is inherent in each of us. Nobody likes when their settled, understandable world, acting according to the learned laws, begins to roll down the drain.

The habit of shifting responsibility for our lives onto the shoulders of others (parents, experts, politicians) explains why we feel helpless in the face of harsh reality. Moreover, we turned everything upside down, calling reality "harsh". It is severe only when we believe that it exists separately from us.

Our whole life has come down to trying to "appease" reality. "Appealing" is achieved by manipulation (in relationships with other people); direct physical, violent influence (striving for immense power) and even spiritual self-development ("I pump Kundalini so that the severity of the world is nothing to me"). Let's go through the stages of development of awareness: To see the self-deception that a person is engaged in.

Self-deception is the ability of the mind to convince you of what you need. For survival, of course. Survival of the physical and social. Social survival should not be underestimated. Man is a social being, dependent on the care and love of other people more than on material comfort. In a society reoriented from relationships to enriching themselves, people feel isolated and lonely. We feel that other people cannot accept us in our entirety, and we begin to manipulate them to get their attention. Hence the overestimated desire for fame, the manual to win the friends of Dale Carnegie, Vedic woman courses and the notorious pickup. Self-deception is the maintenance of a stable sense of "I", and the protection of one's own goodness, and the fencing off of one's motives before the motives of other people (also known as double standards), and inventing assumptions: "he did it because ..." In short, self-deception - This is the story that we push inside daily.

Seeing the world is a big mirror. Have you heard about the projection? Projection is the main way for the One Mind to know itself.

In the same person, different people see completely different sides. We are responding specifically to these sides, and not to the people themselves. In other words, during communication with another person, we do not interact with this person himself, but with those aspects that we project onto him.

A world order where everything around - a mirror image of yourself - is perfectly rational! It helps to see aspects that we do not accept in ourselves (for example, as people who annoy us), and to consciously choose to integrate them.

There are many processes for integrating repressed aspects of oneself. This includes gestalt, working with an inner child, body-oriented therapy, speaking out loud, and regressive hypnosis. The deeper the suppression, the more liberally the work being done.

To find out that everything that happens to you, you pulled to yourself to give yourself the opportunity to develop. In any event, even the most negative, contains a hint to move on. Play the game: observe your emotions throughout the day and ask yourself the question: Thanks to this event, what should I / see? What is my subconscious trying to show me? Which sides of myself do I suppress? What am I afraid to see in myself?

The human body is not a saboteur. Your body is always by your side. Your body is always for you. If you feel uncomfortable inside, your body encourages you to pay attention to what is happening and resolve it. Many injuries continue to surface as emotions first released during the initial injury. A person who is conscious of these emotions notices, sees and "dives" in them, and does not suppress or ignore, putting off life for later.

How to increase efficiency and productivity or how to organize yourself?

If you look at a modern person, it is easy to notice that the speed and complexity of the tasks that now need to be dealt with in life has increased multiply with the volume of tasks that had to be performed 50 years ago.

People are in a hurry, but do not have time. The life of the average person is filled with various messengers, social. networks, email, and dozens of other distractions that crush every day in terms of efficiency and productivity.

Meanwhile, personal effectiveness and productivity - this is the key to success, the level and quality of your life depends on them. In the day only 24 hours. Success is the equivalent of what you manage to do during this time.

Therefore, many dream of the 25th and 26th hours in a day. But in order to succeed, it is not necessary to change the natural chronometer. It is enough to reconsider your approach to work:

- Do not waste your time on meaningless and unimportant things.

Imagine how much time you will have if you exclude routine and unnecessary tasks from your schedule.

- Work on the result. What is your goal? What would you like to achieve by the end of the year? Surprisingly, there are few who can clearly answer these questions. Decide what you want (start a startup, get a promotion, increase earnings, etc.) and confidently go to your goal, devoting at least three hours a day to working on it.

- Cleanliness of the workspace. Put things in order at the workplace.

A cluttered desktop prevents you from focusing, because in an atmosphere of chaos it is difficult to focus your attention on the details of the upcoming work. Tidy up the papers and archive unnecessary folders. This will help you organize your thoughts and effectively complete the task.

The cardinal option is when you just start everything, so to speak, from scratch, changing everything that was, to something that has not been.

Normal option in essence, it is the implementation of a rather strange (at first glance) Buddhist proverb "If you don't like your work, try to love what you are doing." That is, we are talking about changing a sort of subjective approach to activity. In which you, having changed yourself and your perception, are able to discover new, missing sides of the existing work. What, in principle, is possible (and how else would nerds and workaholics exist?), But it requires certain knowledge of skills that are rather difficult to describe here, this is still an article.

Cardinal option.

Firstly, the acceptance and understanding that once having chosen a certain path, you are not obliged to follow it until the end of your life, but rather, you are obliged to periodically review and change it (otherwise you simply lose the freshness of perception and liveliness).

And secondly - you need to work on identifying your own meaning in life according to the algorithm below:

Write down everything that you can do - down to the smallest detail;

Cross out from this list everything that you knowing how to do not like to do;

Cross out from this list what is not paid enough (for you);

What remains should be beneficial to people (cross out all that is useless and harmful);

Write out what is left on a separate sheet and think: - What sphere of life (health, relationships, money, etc.) does this apply to? - What Big Game can and will be carried out? - What professional or social role in this case can be taken? - In what professional field can this be done? - what do you need to master it? - when do you plan to start, and when to finish?

How to get rid of guilt?

Feeling guilty is one of the most difficult to tolerate feelings. Guilt gnaws from the inside, deprives a person of self-confidence, reduces self-esteem. If you turn to the dictionary for the interpretation of the meaning of the word "fault" - an offense, a crime. The culprit is the person who intentionally caused damage or because of criminal negligence. But many people experience a neurotic guilt, and as a rule, those who did not cause harm intentionally. Such people hear an accusing and condemning inner voice, based in most cases on false beliefs.

Choosing "guilt", we unconsciously choose to remain small guilty children and the position of "victim".

Guilt is common for children aged 4-5 years. In adulthood, guilt comes to replace the ability to take responsibility for their actions.

Guilt attracts punishment. As parents punish a child in childhood. It happens that a child becomes so accustomed to "be guilty" and "bear punishment" that he can improve to become good and his parents "loved him" again, which he continues in adulthood to get rid of guilt unconsciously "punish" himself. Punishment can be injuries, losses, illnesses, negative events. Guilt has its positive intentions. This is such a perverted way of getting attention and even love. Again - an unconscious repetition of parent-child relationships. The parent loved and he punished. A bunch of wine-love is formed. And skipping them punishment.

And for someone, guilt is a way to "get better." When a large adult blames a child, he points out a number of his shortcomings, which he tries to correct in order to satisfy the requirements of the parent and receive praise or forgiveness. This pattern of behavior can persist in adulthood. Only an adult has a choice - to grow, develop and improve more environmentally friendly methods. You can try yourself simple ways to get rid of guilt.

Each time, feeling guilty, say to yourself: "I am not to blame (a). I take responsibility for this situation. " Taking responsibility, you can consciously analyze your experience and not repeat the mistake made.

Write down on the sheet the situations when you experienced a very strong sense of guilt and the way in which you managed to "extinguish" this feeling. Try to analyze what "benefit" you have received. Punishment? Attention? An opportunity to avoid liability? Or maybe just out of habit?

Instead of "Excuse me," use "Forgive me." Examples in the picture:

Stop apologizing - start to THANK. A picture with examples is in the photo.   More difficult is the case with unconscious guilt. A person can "punish" himself for many years, destroy his life and health.

- not allow yourself to live at full strength and enjoy life. For example, because of family scenarios:

"My parents worked hard to feed us and denied ourselves everything" - the child grew up, but continues to inherit someone else's model and "refuse everything" to himself. Or punish if you still allow yourself to rest, travel or other pleasures.

"Mom sacrificed her personal life / or career for my sake" - a false conviction makes a person feel an unconscious guilt for their career successes or happiness in their personal lives and, again, unconsciously destroy them so as not to feel guilty about their mom.

"Initiative is punishable" - this belief is more common in men. If guilt is unconscious, then for the realization and resolution of a problem, a person is better off turning to a psychoanalyst for help. Remember that the choice is yours to be the author of your life or a victim of circumstances.